ART AND THE BEAUTY OF GOD

ART
and
THE BEAUTY OF GOD

A Christian Understanding

Richard Harries
Bishop of Oxford

MOWBRAY

Mowbray
A Cassell imprint
Villiers House, 41/47 Strand, London WC2N 5JE
387 Park Avenue South, New York 10016-8810

First published 1993

British Library Cataloguing-in-Publication Data
A catalogue record for this book is available from the British Library.

Library of Congress Cataloging-in-Publication Data
Applied for.

ISBN 0-264-67306-9

Cover photograph of *Christ on a Cross of Lilies* in St Helen's
Church, Abingdon, Oxfordshire by Anthony Burrett

Typeset by Fakenham Photosetting Limited
Printed and bound in Great Britain by Mackays of Chatham PLC

Contents

I am grateful to those who read earlier drafts of this book and who made helpful comments, especially John Drury, Christopher Moody, Ruth McCurry, Piers Plowright, Poh Sim Plowright, Janet Martin Soskice and Oliver Soskice.

Richard Oxon.
January 1993

Acknowledgements

The author and publisher wish to thank the following:
Very Rev. Professor Henry Chadwick, for the extracts from his translation of St Augustine, *Confessions* on pp. x, 6, 36–7, 39, 143 and 145.
Valerie Eliot, for the extract from 'Choruses from "The Rock"' on p. 88.
Faber and Faber Limited, for the extracts from W. H. Auden, 'Meditation on Good Friday' and 'Epistle to a Godson' on pp. 140–2.
Kathleen Raine, for the poem on p. 87, originally published in *The Tablet*.
Acknowledgements for the illustrations appear in the captions.

For the Clergy and People of the Diocese of Oxford

Beauty will save the world.

Dostoevsky, *The Idiot*

In God there is perfect fecundity.

Thomas Aquinas

Artists, in a way, are religious anyway.
They have to be; if by religion one
means believing that life has some
significance, and some meaning, which
is what I think it has. An artist
could not work without believing that.

Henry Moore

Out of Sion hath God appeared in
perfect beauty.

Psalm 50.2

Late have I loved you, beauty so old
and so new.

St Augustine

Faith perishes if it is walled in or
confined. If it is anywhere, it must
be everywhere, like God himself: if
God is in your life, he is in all
things, for he is God. You must be
able to spread the area of your
recognition for him and the basis
of your conviction about him, as
widely as your thought will range.

Austin Farrer

O N E

~~~~~~~~~~~~~~~

The Neglect of Beauty

A t one time the poet Wilfred Owen thought of being ordained. He even worked for a period as lay assistant in the parish of Dunsden. It was not a happy time. When he left he intended to write to the Vicar giving reasons for his dissatisfaction. We do not know whether or not Wilfred Owen wrote that letter but the draft, on the back of an envelope, was found among his papers after his death in France in 1918. It reads: 'To Vicar ... the Christian life affords no imagination, physical sensation, aesthetic philosophy.'[1]

The experience of Wilfred Owen can be paralleled many times over, from both Protestant and Catholic sources. People have found the Christian faith too narrow in its sympathies, inimical to the feelings and stifling to the imagination. In short, it has seemed to afford them no 'aesthetic philosophy'. By this Owen meant no place for beauty, whether in the arts or nature. This is a disaster. For without an affirmation of beauty there can in the end be no faith and no God worth our love.

One of the interesting features of our time is an increasing awareness of the spiritual dimension of the arts. The influential art critic Peter Fuller, who died in 1990 at the age of 42, was in

1

his early life a passionate Marxist. In his last years, however, without ceasing to be an atheist he had become highly critical of a purely materialistic approach to art. As he wrote:

> For myself, I remain an incorrigible atheist; that is my proclamation of faith. Yet there is something about the experience of art, itself, which compels me to re-introduce the category of the 'spiritual'. More than that, I believe that, given the ever-present absence of God, art and the gamut of aesthetic experience, provides the sole remaining glimmer of transcendence. The best we can hope for is that aesthetic surrogate for salvation: redemption through form.

This shift of standpoint was not just personal. As he also wrote:

> One of the most extraordinary features of cultural life in the late 1980s in England was the resurgence of interest in those romantic artists – including Henry Moore, Paul Nash, Stanley Spencer and Cecil Collins – whose contributions usually defy any of the usual materialist 'analyses'.[2]

Peter Fuller uses the word romantic in this passage but the word spiritual would be more appropriate. The artists to whom he refers were consciously spiritual and, in some cases, Christian in their approach. If a religious perspective on life is to carry conviction it has to account for the powerful spiritual impact which the arts, in all forms, have on people. Christianity needs to have a proper place both for the arts and for beauty.

Beauty is one of those big words that modern philosophy tiptoes around. It is also a word that in ordinary conversation is liable to bring up so much gush, what T. S. Eliot termed 'undisciplined squads of emotion', that most people are understandably reticent about its use. Moreover, because experiences of beauty can be intensely emotional, affecting the very core of our being, our understanding of life and who we are, people are extremely reluctant to placard their feelings in public.

The vast majority of us, however, are touched and moved by what strikes us as beautiful, especially in nature. Indeed, for many, it is the experience of the natural world which keeps them sane; which sustains and soothes them in a jarring world. Fishing is the most popular participatory sport in the country with over four million adherents. When I pass a fisherman (it seems to be mostly men) sitting for hour after hour on the river bank catching nothing I cannot believe that they are there just for the fishing. The water, the grass, the calm, the sky: all help to bring peace of heart and mind. In recent years garden centres have become growth businesses and gardening is a major national pastime. Whether it is an allotment, a patio, a window-box or a flowerbed, millions of people find this direct contact with nature therapeutic. Millions more search for beautiful scenes; on car journeys they stop for views, they climb mountains and go for walks. When Alyosha in Dostoevsky's novel *The Brothers Karamazov* saw 'the vault of heaven, full of soft, shining stars, stretched vast and fathomless above him' he

stood, gazed, and suddenly threw himself down on the earth. He did not know why he embraced it. He could not have told why he longed so irresistibly to kiss it, to kiss it all. But he kissed it weeping, sobbing and watering it with his tears, and vowed passionately to love it, and love it for ever and ever. 'Water the earth with the tears of your joy and love those tears' echoed in his soul.[3]

Russians, some think, are given to this kind of emotional rapture, to extremes of feeling. Others of us are more restrained. But because people are private about what affects them most deeply, it should not be assumed that they do not, on occasion, share something of Alyosha's feelings about the beauty of the world.

C. S. Lewis, like Plato and innumerable philosophers influenced by him down the ages, believed that the longing aroused by beauty is a desire for what he called 'our own far-off country' and said that in speaking of this desire even now

> I feel a certain shyness. I am almost committing an indecency. I am trying to rip open the inconsolable secret in each one of you — the secret that hurts so much that you take your revenge on it by calling it names like Nostalgia and Romanticism and Adolescence; the secret also which pierces with such sweetness that when in very intimate conversation, the mention of it becomes imminent, we grow awkward and effect to laugh at ourselves; the secret we cannot hide and cannot tell, though we desire to do both.[4]

What C. S. Lewis describes is an intense feeling, of the utmost significance to those who have experienced it in even a tiny way. If the Christian faith has no understanding of this, or place for it; if it does not have an account of and a value for this sense which is so central to the hidden life of many (perhaps all) it is difficult to see how it can win our allegiance. Like Wilfred Owen we will walk away disgruntled, to write poetry or play music or paint, or simply to enjoy nature, seeing no connection between these activities which sustain and give meaning to our life and what we think of as religion.

The word beauty by itself is not adequate to describe the effect that the arts have on us, as will be discussed in Chapter 4. But it remains an essential aspect of all the arts. (Although it is the visual arts that are often referred to in this book, it is with all the arts that I am concerned.) And it is the arts that engage the most sensitive, serious and creative side of millions today. Despite the feelings of some of those most actively involved in the world of the arts that they are undervalued in our society, they still have great prestige. Pages of the quality newspapers are given over to discussing books, music, films, theatre, opera and so on. Some of this has to do with money and cultural snobbery. But the fact remains that the arts bring not only enjoyment but solace; not only entertainment but inspiration and insight. An enormous amount of classical music is listened to on records and CDs as well as in live concerts. The fact that a new commercial radio station can be entirely devoted to classical music is an indication of a hitherto untapped need. For many, music plays a role that is akin to religion. It stirs our deepest longings and makes us feel that, despite everything, life is worthwhile.

In the nineteenth and early part of the twentieth centuries many of the intelligentsia despised classical religion and valued the arts 'as the evaluation of the soul which, after the vanquishing of religion, is the domain of the educated man', as Paul Tillich put it. He went on to write that:

> In and after the First World War, the belief in the arts as a substitute for religion broke down. Art was not able to open up the sources of power to meet the catastrophes of the twentieth century.[5]

The lecture in which those words were spoken was given in 1952. It was a time of renewed religious faith, particularly in the United States but also in Great Britain. People were still strongly conscious of the Second World War and the need for faith and grace in the face of terrible evil. Since then the arts have to some extent recovered the place they enjoyed amongst the avant-garde intelligentsia in the late nineteenth century. They are once again in danger of becoming a substitute for religion, as the earlier quotation from Peter Fuller made explicit.

As with the experience of beauty in nature, unless the Christian faith has an understanding and place for the arts it will inevitably fail to win the allegiance of those for whom they are the most important aspect of life. For they will see in the Christian faith only what strikes them as flat, moralistic and

5

platitudinous compared to the troubling, haunting depths of Mahler or *King Lear*. Unless the experience of beauty in nature and the arts is encompassed and affirmed the Christian faith will seem to have nothing of interest or importance to say. This is not, however, just a tactic to win the allegiance of the lost. The fact is that God is beautiful and the Church is hiding this. This brings out an even more crucial reason why the concept of beauty must once again play a central role in our understanding of the Christian faith. For without a positive theological evaluation of beauty there is no motive to delight in God and no compelling reason to love him.

Faced with the statement 'You shall love the Lord your God', we can always reply 'Why?' Being told to 'love your neighbour', we can always say 'I choose to do this anyway'. Being told that 'there is a God who made heaven and earth' we can always shrug our shoulders and say 'So what?' The reasons why believers do not make these responses is because we discern in God, the God whose face has shone in the face of Jesus Christ, that which is supremely beautiful. We are drawn, taken out of ourselves, by the one to whom St Augustine addressed the words: 'Late have I loved you, beauty so old and so new.'[6] Augustine was talking about spiritual beauty, the beauty of sublime, self-giving love. But it is central to Christianity, properly understood, that there is a resemblance, a relationship, between the beauty we experience in nature, in the arts, in a genuinely good person and in God; and that which tantalizes, beckons and calls us in beauty has its origin in God himself. So as Hans Urs von Balthasar, the one great modern theologian who has placed beauty at the centre of his theology, puts it:

We can be sure that whoever sneers at her name as if she were the ornament of a bourgeois past — whether he admits it or not — can no longer pray and soon will no longer be able to love.[7]

That sentence is no exaggeration. A sense of beauty and its value, which can of course be part of the experience of the most unlettered person, is an indispensable prerequisite of love and prayer.

In his long poem, 'The Minister', the Welsh priest and poet R. S. Thomas has written:

> Protestantism — the adroit castrator
> Of art; the bitter negation
> Of song and dance and the heart's innocent joy —
> You have botched our flesh and left us only the soul's
> Terrible impotence in a warm world.[8]

This may seem unduly harsh, for there are strains within Protestantism that have not been world-denying or anti-art. Nevertheless, as Wilfred Owen found, the negative attitude inaugurated by many sects at the Reformation and so violently enacted in England in the seventeenth century at the time of Cromwell's Commonwealth, has had a baleful influence. Yet within the total sweep of Christian history, this should be seen as an aberration.

First, the Orthodox Churches have a strong, overriding sense of the beauty of God, which has only rarely been lost sight of. This has been expressed not only in the words of theologians but, no less importantly, through the design and decoration of Byzantine churches. To go into an Orthodox church, with even some of the traditional mosaics or paintings intact, is immediately to be confronted and captivated by a sacrament of the divine beauty. Western mediaeval wall painting was consciously didactic, mostly with a great emphasis on the doom or last judgement. Western Christianity at its worst has been moralistic, and aridly intellectual. The Orthodox Church, without losing sight of the moral dimension or the necessity of spiritual discipline, puts before us a vision of the beauty of God, radiant in Christ, shining in the saints and beginning to glimmer in us.

At the height of the Cold War I once spoke to a young priest in Moscow about his spiritual pilgrimage. He told me he had been brought up by atheistic parents and inculcated with atheism at school. But, he said, the imprint of Marxism could not stamp everything. He came across the music and icons of the Russian Orthodox Church and through their beauty was led to the truth.

Secondly, even in Western Christianity, especially in the era of the undivided Church, beauty was a leading theme and dimension of Christian thinking, one which was well able to encompass and inspire great art. Indeed, as one of the best-known atheists of our time, Marghanita Laski, once put it:

> Since the Renaissance ... it's been all too sadly apparent that in all the arts there has been no inspiration comparable with the inspiration that religion gave. There have been no words for secular music to compare with the music of a Mass. I certainly think that belief in God and the religions that arose from belief in God did give a shaping and a pattern to life for which I can see no conceivable substitute.[9]

Hans Urs von Balthasar points up the place of beauty in the Western tradition by focusing on the works of Irenaeus, Augustine, Denys, Anselm and Bonaventure. Whilst acutely aware of the neglect of beauty in Roman Catholic theology in recent centuries, he nevertheless finds this concern present in the work of lay people, such as Dante, St John of the Cross, Pascal, Soloviev, Hopkins and Péguy. Now, in part due to the publication of Balthasar's work and its translation into English, there is a revival of interest in this neglected, but essential dimension of Christian truth.

Travellers in the Mediterranean are struck by the beauty of ancient Greek and Roman art. They are moved by the Parthenon and other temples, by Greek statues and Roman busts. It seems that it was not until the fifth century, when the

Byzantine Emperor Justinian commissioned churches and mosaics in Ravenna, that Christianity appeared as a flame of beauty in the world. But this is deceptive. Art in the Greco-Roman world was associated with paganism. It is understandable that the Christian Church in its infant years should want nothing to do with it. Furthermore, during the first three centuries of its existence the Church was, from time to time, savagely persecuted. Christians, unless they wanted to face martyrdom, which some did, needed to keep a low profile. So although Christians did draw and paint, as we know from the moving depictions in the catacombs at Rome and elsewhere, which date from the second and third centuries, these cannot really be classed as works of art, fascinating and moving though they are. When in the fourth century, under the Emperor Constantine, Christianity became first allowed and then the official religion of the Roman world, beautiful churches were built, mosaics were made and icons were painted. But it is totally false to think that before the fourth century Christians had no sense of beauty.

The first Christians were overwhelmed with a sense of the beauty of a God who came amongst us as one poor and lowly, to help the poor and lowly achieve eternal salvation. The overwhelming sense of spiritual beauty was expressed primarily in literary rather than visual terms at that stage. There was, first, the early Christian appreciation of the Hebrew Scriptures. There is wonderful poetry in the Hebrew Bible, both in the Psalms and elsewhere. There are many different kinds of literary skill: narrative, descriptive, rhythmic and so on. The first Christians also had the sayings and parables of Christ passed on to them. The parables are themselves a superb art form, encapsulating in a short and vivid way some truth which, with dramatic irony, forces the listener or hearer to question themselves. Each of the Gospels is written from a particular perspective, with its own literary form and shape. The Gospel according to St John is one of the world's great works of art. A few years ago Lord Eccles wrote a book describing how, though he was an agnostic, he was drawn into the biblical world through its literary quality, especially the Gospel of St John. He was amazed that the Church ignored the literary excellence of its tradition.

The complex, mutually fruitful interaction of religious and literary texts is one of the most promising areas of present study. George Steiner has written:

> Something fascinating is happening to literary criticism. Literary scholars, students of poetics, textual commentators and critics, are reverting openly to religious concerns ... Once again it is as if 'The Good Book' is being felt to be the archetype of 'good books' in general and of the complex means whereby our imaginations experience the life of the world.

I have mentioned the Gospel of St John as one of the great works of art. A. D. Nuttall, when Professor of English at Sussex University, examined the conversation of Jesus and Pilate in John 18.33–38. He judged it to be a remarkably early specimen of what literary critics called 'discontinuous dialogue'. 'The usual story told by scholars of drama is that the discontinuous dialogue in favour with the epigoni of Harold Pinter really began with Chekhov', he wrote. He then goes on to suggest that it is present in the Johannine dialogue. The early Christians had a strong and distinctive sense of beauty, one which I hope to bring out in subsequent chapters. Nevertheless, it is impossible to deny that from time to time in the Church there has been some sheer Philistinism. It was this which Wilfred Owen experienced in his vicar and which made R. S. Thomas react so bitterly in the poem already quoted. If, as I believe, with Balthasar, that a sense of beauty is essential for belief in God, it is important to expose the enemies of beauty. The main enemy is cliché in all its forms. One of the themes, which I set out more fully in Chapter 4, is that beauty is inseparable from truth and goodness. Indeed, beauty is the persuasive power of God's truth and goodness. So beauty is in the end about honesty, about seeing what is actually there and being true to one's own response to it. Cliché, whether verbal or visual, takes what is unthought out, unfelt, in short, acceptable at a superficial level. But all apprehension of beauty involves a struggle to apprehend the truth and all artistic creation involves a struggle to express it. Arnold Bennett once wrote:

> You have said sometimes to yourself, 'If only I could write.' You were wrong. You ought to have said, 'If only I could think and feel.' ... When you cannot express yourself, depend upon it that you have nothing precise to express, but what incommodes you is not the vain desire to express yourself better but the vain desire to think more clearly, and to feel more deeply.

People sometimes ask for simple gospel truths. Too often, however, what they have in mind are the pious platitudes of a previous generation. True simplicity is indeed a highly prized virtue. But it does not come by opening a packet. After a lifetime of thinking, struggling, loving and praying we might, through the grace of God, have achieved true simplicity.

The other failure has to do with the moral sensibility. A novelist once wrote about her work: get the tone right and everything else follows. The tone has to do with an awareness of who it is that one is communicating to, in what circumstances. If, metaphorically, it is a shout when it should be a whisper, a hectoring when it should be diffident pleading, then all is failure. This in the end has to do with sensitivity, with a human capacity to recognize real people and the actual feel of life. This requires attention to the particular as well as the general. There is a proper place for the general, for the abstract and speculative, for doctrine and philosophy. But too often the

Church has offered premature conclusions, and has failed to grasp the actual texture of human existence. The result is that people's moral instincts react against the kind of picture of God which is being conveyed to them. It simply does not convince or it arouses the moral hackles. The Church needs modern liturgies and there is no reason why they should not have the quality of some liturgies of the past. But they will not have this quality if they are simply a pastiche of acceptable phrases. The Church needs good sermons and there is no reason why there should not be good sermons today as in the past. But these will not be produced without a great deal more honesty. One of the most remarkable religious publications this century was the book of sermons by Harry Williams entitled *The True Wilderness*. This spoke to millions because, as he avowed, there came a point in his life when he was unwilling to preach anything that was not true to his own experience. The truth that he conveyed in those sermons often had great beauty; and they were directed towards the production of genuine goodness. Beauty is the product of honest attention to the particular. And though sometimes the enemies of beauty have had their way in the Church, yet there is more than enough to encourage us.

For much of European history the Church has been the biggest patron of the arts, encouraging beauty as well as godliness. Since the Romantic Movement in the early nineteenth century, however, religion and beauty have sometimes been seen as rivals. This is in part the fault of Christians and Christian institutions. But there is a potential within all love of beauty and the arts for this to become a rival to faith. Aestheticism can reign, the pursuit of beauty for its own sake unrelated to other values. The arts can become self-sufficient or concerned only with prestige, intellectual or financial. The Christian suspicion of beauty and the arts which is expressed from time to time, is not entirely the result of a lack of appreciation.

Something of the tension engendered by these considerations

can be seen, for example, in Evelyn Waugh. Waugh had a well-developed aesthetic sense, particularly a visual one. At school he designed bookplates and took some training in order to become an artist. Yet when he converted to Roman Catholicism he went to some trouble to emphasize that this was in response to the truth, as he saw it, not where his aesthetic inclinations might naturally have led him. For he was quite clear that the Roman Catholic trappings of the 1930s, the design of churches and their ornaments, the music and the liturgy, were inferior to the Anglicanism in which he had been brought up. Sometimes he takes an almost perverse delight in stressing the cheapness or tawdriness of some Roman Catholic artefact. Right at the end of *Brideshead Revisited*, at what is the culminating point of the novel, Charles Ryder meditates before the Blessed Sacrament. Waugh writes: 'A small red flame — a beaten-copper lamp of deplorable design re-lit before the beaten-copper doors of the tabernacle.' Here the focus of faith, Christ in the Blessed Sacrament, co-exists with a lamp of deplorable design, but that design in no way undermines the truth of the faith. It would seem we have a total disjunction between beauty and truth. Yet the other pole is also suggested in *Brideshead Revisited*. At the beginning, Charles, then an agnostic, says to Sebastian about the Christmas story: 'But my dear Sebastian, you can't seriously *believe* it all.' 'Oh yes', replies Sebastian, 'It's a lovely idea.' Charles protests, 'But you can't believe things because they're a lovely idea.' 'But I *do*', responds Sebastian, 'That's how I believe.'[10] Christian truth is not dependent upon earthly forms of beauty. For Christ can be known as we serve his run-down brothers and sisters in the most squalid surroundings. Spiritual beauty can be discerned there. Yet that spiritual beauty can also shine in a special way through human beauty and artistic creation. In the traditional Christmas story spiritual beauty and artistic beauty coalesce.

Another who felt the tension was Robert Browning. In his long poem 'Christmas Eve and Easter Day' of 1850 he imagines himself in a chapel of poor worshippers. He is repelled by the sight and smell of the people and the ignorance of the preacher. He leaves and in his mental pilgrimage goes to the beauties of Rome and the intellectual questioning of Göttingen:

> I thought it best that thou, the spirit,
> Be worshipped in spirit and in truth,
> And in beauty, as even we require it —
> Not in the forms of burlesque, uncouth,
> I left but now, as scarcely fitted
> For Thee.

In the end, however, neither the artistic works of Rome nor the intellectual heights of German Protestantism satisfy him. In mystical vision he meets Christ and returns to that chapel of simple, sincere folk, drab and ugly though they might be and appalling the preacher.

> It were to be wished the flaws were fewer
> In the earthen vessel, holding treasure
> Which lies as safe in a golden ewer;
> But the main thing is, does it hold good measure?
> Heaven soon sets right all other matters! —
> Ask, else, these ruins of humanity,
> This flesh worn out to rags and tatters,
> This soul that struggles with insanity,
> Who thence take comfort — can I doubt?[11]

Yet, that said, Browning was a poet and sought to express his faith in and through his poetic skills. These he set to struggle with and serve truth, but a truth adorned with beauty. For he, no less than we, could give up the idea that beauty is one of God's gifts and artistic beauty has its origin in him.

When the love of beauty and the love of God come together the result can be powerful indeed. It is usual to see the religious

14

revival which we term the Oxford Movement as part of the wider Romantic Movement which swept the whole of Europe. One aspect of this, from a religious point of view, was a new appreciation of the role of the aesthetic in religious life. One of the genuinely holy, humble men of the Oxford Movement was John Keble. Nobody would ever accuse him of pursuing beauty for its own sake. Yet he was quite clear that there was an essential kinship between beauty and religious truth. As Professor of Poetry at Oxford from 1832 to 1841 he delivered 40 lectures exploring the nature of poetry and its relationship to religion. He believed that they were allies, that there was a hidden bond between them. Both sought to express thoughts and feelings beyond the power of prose to describe. Each had something to offer the other. Keble believed that in both religion and poetry there is something that draws us but that this profound spiritual attractiveness leads us on gently.

> Religion and poetry are akin because each is marked by a pure reserve, a kind of modesty or reverence. To follow nature sensitively, you need to follow her unveiling part of herself. You are led upwards from beauty to beauty, quietly and serenely, step by step, with no sudden leap from depths to height. Beauty is shy, is not like a man rushing out in front of a crowd. Religion too, if it is wise, models itself upon the ways of Scripture, where the treasure of truth is hidden from the idle and unready, to be seen only when the eye of the mind is pure.[12]

Although the taste of the first generation of the Oxford Movement was simple, unadorned, even austere by our standards, subsequent generations beautified churches and sought to make the worship of the Church beautiful precisely because, like Keble, they loved beauty and saw in earthly beauty the glow of divine beauty.

Those who lament the demise of the Book of Common Prayer

or the Authorized Version of the Bible have a point in their conviction that religious truth can and should take beautiful forms. We need not think, however, whatever the banality of some modern expressions, that beauty is banished from the Church today. The longing is always there, seeking new forms. We need think only of Coventry Cathedral and the special works commissioned for it, the works of Matisse and Chagall which adorn a number of churches. Sadly, there have been few like Dean Hussey, who commissioned works by Britten and Moore as well as by several leading painters. But there have been some. Surveying the period from 1940 to 1990 in Britain Tom Devonshire-Jones concludes his catalogue of exhibitions, publications, individuals and locations with the judgement that 'the interest that art and theology have shown in one another has ebbed and flowed. The present is a time full of hope for increase in understanding.'[13]

Plato has an interesting passage in which he contrasts the lustre of beauty with the lack of a similar lure in the moral sphere.

> Now the earthly likenesses of justice and self-discipline and all the other forms which are precious to souls keep no lustre, and there are few who by the use of their feeble faculties and with great difficulty can recognize in the counterface the family likeness of the originals. But beauty was once ours to see in all its brightness ... beauty shone bright in the world above, and here too it still gleams clearest.[14]

Plato accounts for the attractiveness of what is beautiful by his belief that the soul experiences the reality of beauty — beauty in itself, the ideal form of beauty — before birth and still remembers this on earth. Most Christians (the second-century theologian Origen was an exception) could not go along with this explanation. Nevertheless the phenomenon itself is still with us. It is worth reflecting on and needs integrating into our overall view of the world. Beauty 'still gleams clearest'. Moral principles are vital, yet so often we have to drive ourselves to do what is right. Beauty, on the other hand, haunts us. It draws and compels and gives. Why? If I did not believe that God is the source and standard of all that I experience as beautiful, that he/she is beauty as much as truth and goodness, I would not be a religious believer at all. Indeed, on the basis of what I have said I not only would not; in principle, I could not be a believer in any real sense. I might respond to God as a great commander-in-chief but I could not give myself to him as the goal of all my longing and my supreme delight. When Mother Teresa of Calcutta began making a film with Malcolm Muggeridge, she wrote to him the words 'Now let us do something beautiful for God'. She wanted to do something beautiful because she believes God, in his love, to be supreme beauty. It is this beauty that draws her to do something beautiful in response. It is also quite clear from her example that a strong sense of beauty need not detract us from a firm moral commitment to those in need. God is the goal of all our longing. But before this theme is pursued it is necessary to explore more closely what might be meant by using the word beauty at all.

Notes

1 Jon Stallworthy, *Wilfred Owen: A Biography* (OUP, 1974), p. 86.

2 Peter Fuller, *Images of God* (Chatto & Windus, 1990), new Foreword.

3 F. Dostoevsky, *The Brothers Karamazov* (Penguin, 1958), vol. II, p. 426.

4 C. S. Lewis, 'The Weight of Glory' in *Transposition and Other Addresses* (Bles, 1949), p. 23.

5 *Paul Tillich on Art and Architecture*, ed. John and Jane Dillenberger (Crossroad, New York, 1987), p. 27.

6 St Augustine, *Confessions*, trans. Henry Chadwick (OUP, 1992), p. 201.

7 Hans Urs von Balthasar, *The Glory of the Lord*, vol. 1 (T. & T. Clark, 1982), p. 18.

8 R. S. Thomas, 'The Minister' in *Song at the Year's Turning* (Rupert Hart-Davis, 1955), p. 92.

9 Anthony Bloom with Marghanita Laski, *God and Man* (Darton, Longman and Todd, 1971), p. 29.

10 Evelyn Waugh, *Brideshead Revisited* (Penguin, 1964), pp. 331, 84.

11 Robert Browning, 'Christmas Eve and Easter Day' in *Poems* (World Classics, OUP, 1952), pp. 291ff.

12 John Keble, *Praelectiones Academicae*, trans. Owen Chadwick in *The Mind of the Oxford Movement* (A. & C. Black, 1963), pp. 70-1.

13 Tom Devonshire-Jones, 'Art-Theology-Church, a Survey 1940-1990 in Britain', *Theology* (September-October 1992).

14 Plato, *Phaedrus* (Penguin, 1973), p. 57.

T W O

∾∾∾∾∾∾∾∾∾∾∾

What Is Beauty?

When I was a parish priest I visited a parishioner in hospital. Her body was so wasted away she hardly made a bump under the bedclothes. She was nearly blind. After the initial greetings were over she suddenly said, 'Tell me, Father, what *is* beauty?' I rejoiced that despite the decrepitude of the body her mind was still so active and I reflected with her on this age-old question. She was a former headmistress, educated in the Classics, and the question with which Plato and so many others have struggled she still found interesting. But whoever we are and wherever we live, the question 'What is beauty?' is important. We use the word about pictures and people, music and mountains. What do we mean by it?

If we look at a great painting, say *The Baptism of Christ* by Piero della Francesca in the National Gallery, it is possible to pick out certain characteristics that contribute to its beauty. It has, for example, a delectable harmony. Most obviously there are vertical and horizontal lines that intersect at right angles. The tree, Christ, his praying hands, the water flowing from the bowl, the beak of the dove, and John the Baptist's right leg carry

19

the eye up and down the picture. The hands of the angels and John the Baptist, the wings of the dove and the clouds in the sky float the eyes sideways and intersect the vertical lines at a number of points. But a series of right angles would be of little visual interest, so there are also harmoniously balanced diagonals, formed by the left leg of John the Baptist, the back of the man undressing, the silhouette of the hills and so on. Again, if the picture was divided down the middle it would be dull, but the artist wished to have different sections. So the position of the tree makes the actual baptism the major focus, whilst the space in this section is related in a proportionate way to that behind the tree where the angels stand. An analysis of the blends and contrasts of colours could also be carried out showing how they fit together in an interesting and arresting whole. In short, in every aspect there is harmony, balance, proportion; what ancient writers called 'symmetry' and 'measure'.

At the same time, the painting as a whole adds up to a satisfying unity but again in a way which is no stereotype. The curve at the top of the painting, the leaves of the tree and the combination of trees and water help to make the details cohere. The parts balance one another and contribute to the whole.

There is another feature we can easily recognize, the use of light. The body of Christ and the flesh tones of the other people in the picture have an extraordinary translucence. Similarly the bark of the tree, the water and the sky stand out in an almost unearthly light. There is, we might say, a radiance about the scene.

Not every painting or work of art yields so easily to this analysis. Nevertheless it is easy to understand why St Thomas Aquinas (1225–74) selected wholeness, harmony and radiance as the three defining characteristics of what is beautiful.[1] For these are the three most obvious characteristics that emerge, whether we look at a classical work like Piero della Francesca's *The Baptism of Christ* or a modern one like Bridget Riley's *Daybreak*. They are characteristics that are as applicable to sculpture and architecture as they are to painting. This understanding is one that draws on the long tradition of classical and Christian thinking on the subject. Robert Grosseteste, Bishop of Lincoln and scholar with a wide range of interests who, like Thomas Aquinas, lived in the thirteenth century, had this conception of beauty:

> For beauty is a concordance and fittingness of a thing to itself and of all its individual parts to themselves and to each other and to the whole, and of that whole to all things.[2]

It is true that some thinkers have wanted to modify or enlarge the definition of beauty in terms of symmetry and measure. Plotinus, the third-century philosopher who has been such an enormous influence on Christian thinkers, did not think the beauty of light could fit into this definition.

> Almost everyone declares that the symmetry of parts towards each other and towards a whole, with, besides, a certain charm of colour, constitutes the beauty recognized by the eye, that invisible things, as indeed in all else, universally, the beautiful thing is essentially symmetrical, patterned. But think what this means. Only a compound can be beautiful, never anything devoid of parts ... all the loveliness of colour and even the light of the sun, being devoid of parts and so not beautiful by symmetry, must be ruled out of the realm of beauty.[3]

We might take other examples: that of the modern picture which consists simply of one colour all over the canvas, or a clear blue sky. How can these simple wholes without parts be regarded as beautiful by the traditional definition? For Grosseteste, however, a simple unity was itself the best of all forms.

> Light is beautiful in itself, for its nature is simple and all things

21

are like to it. Wherefore it is integrated in the highest degree and most harmoniously proportioned and equal to itself: for beauty is a harmony of proportions.[4]

What applies to light, he regarded as applying even more to God: 'For God is supremely simple, supremely concordant and appropriate to himself.'

The example of a painting has been given in order to show the strength of Aquinas's understanding of beauty as that which has wholeness, harmony and radiance. But every work of art has form of one kind or another. Poetry makes use of metre, rhythm and rhyme; a novel has a beginning, a middle and an end and a host of subtle interconnections, parallels, echoes and contrasts in the text; and so on. Forms can and do change: as when Wilfred Owen made more use of half-rhymes, assonance and internal rhyming; as when Hopkins developed his sprung rhythm and Eliot reacted against Georgian poetry. But form there must be and without form there is no work of art. Forms vary enormously. But it is the form which distinguishes a painting from a splurge of paint, music from a cacophony of sound, a novel or play from a rambling anecdote. In them all, the details relate to one another and the whole in a way which achieves a satisfying unity. There is wholeness and harmony.

I recognize that for some the emphasis on wholeness, harmony and radiance will point to what is pretty rather than what is beautiful. However, beautiful works of art often include that which is disturbing and ugly, dark and disruptive. They can express violence, evoke sorrow and depict the sordid. This is an important point which I fully accept. There is the world of difference between superficial prettifying and genuine beauty. But, as I argue later in Chapter 4, beauty to be beauty must always be seen in integral relation to truth. It is this which allows it to express or include all that seems the opposite of what is whole, harmonious and radiant. But for the sake of clarity of terms I believe that the word beauty should be

22

associated with the particular characteristics of form that I have outlined: wholeness and harmony.

There is also radiance, though this needs to be interpreted more widely than physical light. It includes illumination of all kinds: intellectual, moral and spiritual. Works of art not only satisfy the senses, they bring insight and challenge. This understanding is also deeply embedded in the European tradition.

What I am suggesting is that when we describe a scene in nature or a work of art as being beautiful, there are certain definite features that can be recognized and discussed. This view is in sharp contrast to the one so widely held in the modern world that 'beauty is in the eye of the beholder'; that beauty is entirely a matter of personal taste and there is nothing objective about it. It is obvious that people often disagree about what they find beautiful but the very fact that when such disagreements occur we can talk, put forward reasons for our judgements, be understood and perhaps modify our views somewhat, indicates some shared criteria of judgement. As in the case of disagreement over moral issues, the very fact that we can discourse with those whose views are different from our own indicates the existence of some common ground.

Some great art has a capacity to appeal to every culture and every age. The Taj Mahal, that magnificent monument of Mogul architecture, seems miraculously to fulfil the expectations of everyone who looks at it. However often seen it never disappoints. Nevertheless some art of other cultures does strike us as alien or ugly. Europeans do not always respond to statues of Hindu gods and goddesses or Japanese drama. This suggests that perceptions of beauty are culturally conditioned. They are certainly culturally shaped. But this need not imply that the criteria of beauty in different cultures are totally different. For people in one culture can and do come to appreciate the works of art of another. Japanese Nō theatre is a good example. To people brought up in the tradition of European theatre this does at first seem extremely strange. Yet both W. B. Yeats and Benjamin Britten were influenced by it. The spareness of Nō drama, with its single tree on stage, the ritual aspect and the slight changes in sound or movement which indicate a major shift in mood, can come to be appreciated for its very austereness. All art depends on the human capacity to appreciate and discriminate. This is a process of education and development. The capacity to appreciate the art of another culture is not essentially different from the capacity to appreciate an innovation in the arts of our own. Such innovations are almost invariably greeted by a lack of understanding and rejection before being acclaimed and integrated into the tradition.

Tastes change from age to age and this again leads us to think that beauty must be subjective, dependent on the cultural outlook of a particular time. Tastes do indeed change. The Gothic Revival in the nineteenth century now appears to us in a much more favourable light than it did fifty years ago, in part thanks to people like John Betjeman. Archaic art, that is Greek art of the sixth century BC as opposed to the classical art which came later, is valued by us more than by our Victorian forebears, in part owing to the influence of critics like Clive Bell. The examples are endless. But while it remains true that each age has a special feel for some kinds of art, it is absurd arrogance for any one generation to disdain what has been appreciated by former generations. It is not only absurd, it is also damaging. We are only now beginning to realize the full extent of the damage done by Victorian restorers to eighteenth-century and earlier work, which we now recognize has its own special appeal. Two principles can guide us. First, there are many different kinds of beauty and whilst all forms will be characterized by wholeness, harmony and radiance, they will have these attributes in different ways. It is quite possible to appreciate many different kinds of art: to be moved by the mosques of the architect Sinan in Istanbul as well as the Gothic cathedrals of England; to delight in the fifteenth-century tiles from Iznik as well as in a Chippendale chair. People who love Mahler are quite capable of enjoying Vivaldi as well, and the popularity of both in our time does not necessarily indicate two totally different groups of people.

Secondly, what is truly beautiful will over time establish itself as such. Fashions change but in the long run a tradition is formed, in which a variety of excellences can be appreciated. It was Byzantine art that set the standard for Christian civilization for a thousand years. Vasari, the sixteenth-century art critic and painter, in extolling the virtues of the Renaissance contrasted these favourably with what he thought of as primitive Greek art. It was a view widely shared in the nineteenth century and promulgated by people like Ruskin. We do not now share this view. Byzantine art, especially in the form of icons which are increasingly popular, has its own form of spiritual and aesthetic appeal. But in valuing Byzantine art, this does not mean to say that we necessarily lose all appreciation for the artistic achievements of the Renaissance.

The 'objective' view of beauty put forward here will strike some as over-intellectual and cold, as not doing justice to the intense feelings aroused by our experiences of beauty. I readily admit that what strikes us as beautiful does indeed arouse powerful feelings; feelings of pleasure, delight, wonder and longing. But the presence of such feelings are not in themselves grounds for ascribing beauty to the object which evokes them. Such feelings are the effect which something beautiful has on us. They are the results of beauty, not part of its defining characteristics. Beauty may arouse a sense of delight, but that sense of delight itself cannot be taken as an indication that what evoked it is to be described as beautiful. Sometimes beauty reduces people to tears, as it did Alyosha in the quotation from Dostoevsky. But we cry for many reasons, few of them connected with the experience of beauty. Beauty gives us pleasure but so does a dish of raspberries. So the fact that we feel certain sensations when we experience beauty cannot be part of the anatomy of beauty. Nevertheless, the feelings aroused are indeed significant and distinctive, indicating an important aspect of Christian truth, which I will explore in Chapter 7.

From the earliest stages of the discussion of beauty philosophers have been conscious that the word beauty is used both about aspects of the created, physical world and about the immaterial, spiritual realm. It is not only a flower that can be called beautiful but a soul. We still today sometimes talk about a lovely person. Indeed it is the central thrust of Plato, Plotinus, Augustine and others that we should seek the higher beauty. We should move on from an appreciation of the beauty of the body to the beauty of the soul, from the beauty of the earth to the beauty of the intelligible world. All this is a prelude to discerning the source and standard of beauty in beauty itself, as a Platonist would say, or in God as a Christian would put it. But can we really use the same word beauty about all these different realities?

Patrick Sherry, the author of a recent introduction to theological aesthetics, points out that we are quite familiar with the use of the word beauty for non-material realities, for example when we talk about a mathematical theorem or the plot of a novel being beautiful.[5] He argues in favour of a cross-categorial relationship. People often make cross-categorial comparisons, for instance when they speak of colourful music or the sweetness of various kinds of art. The word colour, normally used of physical objects, is used for sound. The word sweetness, used for tastes, is applied to that which is seen or touched. The great American Puritan thinker Jonathan Edwards said of the world that 'the sweetest and most charming beauty of it is its resemblance of spiritual beauties ... how great a resemblance of the holy and virtuous soul is a calm serene day'.[6] In a similar way Sherry argues that the word beauty may validly be used about a range of realities that would normally be placed in different categories. There is a family relationship between the various uses.

In his recent book Matthew Fox sums up, in dialogue form, the thought of Thomas Aquinas. Part of the dialogue reads:

Aquinas: Just as art is manifested through the work of the artist, so God's wisdom is manifested through creatures. (Wisdom 13.5: 'For from the greatness and beauty of created things, their original author by analogy is seen.')

Fox: You have used the term 'beauty' frequently in our conversation. In what way is 'beauty' an important dimension of a spiritual relationship to creation?

Aquinas: The highest beauty is in the Godhead, since beauty consists in comeliness: but God is beauty itself, beautifying all things. The Creator of beauty has set up all the beauty of things. Divinity is manifest through the names of Wise and Beautiful. Dionysius says that theologians praise God as 'wise and beautiful', since all beings ... 'are full of every divine harmony', that is, they exist with perfect consonance or order from God and are full 'with a holy beauty'. When he says 'harmony', he is alluding to wisdom, a characteristic of which is to order and measure things. When there is something lacking in harmony or beauty, corruption occurs in things, an excess of their proper nature takes over. This happens with disease in bodies and with sin in the soul.

Fox: You are saying, then, that beauty and wisdom go together?

Aquinas: Dionysius teaches that the supersubstantial 'Good' that is God 'is praised by the holy theologians' in sacred Scripture 'as the beautiful'. (Song of Songs 1.15: 'Behold, you are beautiful, my love.')

Fox: Thus, beauty and goodness go together. You have said that every being is good. Is every being also beautiful? What about beauty in God and in creatures?

Aquinas: Beauty and goodness in a thing are identical fundamentally ... and consequently goodness is praised as beauty. But they differ logically, for goodness properly relates to the appetite, while beauty relates to the cognitive faculty: for beautiful things are those that please when seen. Thus beauty consists in due proportion — for the senses delight in due proportion, as in what is after their own kind, because even sense is a sort of reason, just as is every cognitive faculty.

The beautiful and beauty are attributed in different ways to God and to creatures. In God, as Dionysius says, 'the beautiful and beauty must not be divided', as if the beautiful were one thing in God and beauty another.

Fox: And for creatures?

Aquinas: Dionysius says that 'in existing things' the beautiful and beauty are distinguished as the sharer and the shared, so that 'the beautiful' is said to be 'that which participates in beauty'; but beauty is a sharer in the first Cause, which makes all things 'beautiful'. For the beauty of a creature is nothing other than a likeness of the divine beauty sharing all things.[7]

For a Christian the justification of using the word beauty about both physical and spiritual realities is derived not simply from an analysis of the way such words are used but from a theological view of the world. From a Christian view the physical and the spiritual both find their fount and origin in God, the giver of all good things. So now I want to look more closely at the beauty of God and the beauty of the world, in order to explore the relationship between them.

Notes

1 Thomas Aquinas, *Summa Theologica*, 1a, XXXIX. 8.

    For beauty includes three conditions, *integritas sive perfectio* (integrity or wholeness), *debita proportio sive consonantia* (right proportion or harmony) and *claritas* (radiance).

2 Robert Grosseteste, quoted by Umberto Eco, *Art and Beauty in the Middle Ages* (Yale, 1986), p. 48.

3 Plotinus, *The Enneads*, i. 6. I (Penguin, 1991), p. 46.

4 *Art and Beauty in the Middle Ages*, p. 49.

5 Patrick Sherry, *Spirit and Beauty* (OUP, 1992), pp. 150-5. This is a helpful book for those who wish to pursue the subject of theological aesthetics further.

6 Jonathan Edwards, quoted by Sherry, op. cit.

7 Matthew Fox OP, *Sheer Joy: Conversations with Thomas Aquinas on Creation Spirituality* (HarperCollins, 1992), pp. 102-3.

T H R E E

∾∾∾∾∾∾∾∾∾∾∾∾

The Beauty of God and the Beauty of the World

W hy should we attribute beauty to God? Plato believed that in everything that strikes us as beautiful there is a beauty which participates in the ideal beauty (the idea or form of beauty itself). We should therefore move on quickly through lower manifestations of beauty to the supreme beauty from which all emanates. Plato's most famous expression of this view is given by Diotima in *The Symposium*. A person must begin by applying himself to contemplation of physical beauty, first by falling in love with one particular beautiful person and then by noting the resemblances between that beauty and beauty in other people.

The next stage is for him to reckon beauty of soul more valuable than beauty of body; the result will be that, when he encounters a virtuous soul in a body which has little of the bloom of beauty, he will be content to love and cherish it and to bring forth such notions as will serve to make young people better.

He will then begin to see that all beauty is akin and will discern

31

beauty not only in the moral realm but in the sciences. So he will begin to grasp the vast ocean of intellectual beauty.

The man who has been guided thus far in the mysteries of love, and who has directed his thoughts towards examples of beauty in due and orderly succession, will suddenly have revealed to him as he approaches the end of his initiation a beauty whose nature is marvellous indeed, the final goal, Socrates, of all his efforts. This beauty is first of all eternal; it neither comes into being nor passes away, neither waxes or wanes; next, it is not beautiful in part and ugly in part, nor beautiful at one time and ugly at another, nor beautiful in this relation and ugly in that, nor beautiful here and ugly there, as varying according to its beholders; ... he will see it as absolute, existing alone with itself, unique, eternal, and all other beautiful things as partaking of it, yet in such a manner that, while they come into being and pass away, it neither undergoes any increase or diminution or suffers any change.[1]

Plato's theory of forms, as it is called, has been criticized from Aristotle onwards. In the physical world we do not think that there is any one ideal; one ideal bed, for example, to which all others must conform and in which every well-designed bed will share. There are many different designs of bed, excellent in their different ways. Nor can we readily see that abstract nouns like truth, beauty and goodness exist of themselves in an ideal, intelligible world. They are words that we use to describe the qualities of people and things. Nevertheless, many Christians (including most Christian philosophers and theologians until Aquinas, and many after) have had a deep sympathy with Plato and sought to respond to what they sensed to be a genuine religious impulse. This impulse was given full religious expression by Plotinus, who has been more influential on Christian thinking than even Plato himself.

Plotinus, basing his thinking on Diotima's speech and the

myth of Phaedrus, in which the soul mounts to heaven in a chariot, grounded Plato's philosophical thrust in a reality which was unequivocably spiritual. This beauty induces 'wonderment and delicious trouble, longing and love and a trembling that is all delight'. And someone who has this vision

> With what passion of love shall he not be seized, with what pang of desire, with what longing to be molten into one with This, what wondering delight! If he that has never seen this Being must hunger for It as for all his welfare, he that has known must love and reverence it as the very beauty; he will be flooded with awe and gladness, stricken by a salutory terror; he loves with a veritable love, with sharp desire; all other loves than this he must despise, and disdain, all that once seemed fair.[2]

Finally, the thought of Plotinus was well and truly baptized by Augustine of Hippo (354–430), who in his *Confessions* especially, but also elsewhere, echoes him. Indeed, for a period before becoming a Christian Augustine was himself a Neo-Platonist and it was Neo-Platonism which took him a significant way towards Christianity.

Although Plato's system has been subjected to much philosophical criticism, anyone with any spark of religious feeling is bound to be sympathetic to it for two closely related reasons. First, God is the giver of all good gifts. Everything which we value in this life has its source and standard in him. We value experiences of earthly beauty, so these must have their origin in a divine generosity which itself has the character of beauty. Yet, we might argue, sport is valuable and this does not lead us to think of God as a divine sportsman. We prize good cooking but we are not thereby led to picture God as a divine chef. Analogies drawn from sport or cooking might be applicable to certain aspects of God's relation to us. But, we want to say, beauty belongs to the nature or very essence of God, as does

33

truth and goodness. This leads on to the second, related reason for sympathy with the thrust of Plato's thinking. God contains within himself all perfections. Physical prowess and culinary techniques belong to finite existence. So far as we know they have no place in heaven. But beauty, as we have seen, is a term that can be applied to non-material realities and it is an aspect of all that we value (even sport and cooking). If there was a divine power that existed without beauty we could think of a much more worthy object of our worship, namely one which was beautiful, one who has beauty in supreme, surpassing degree.

This train of thought is not intended to prove that such a God exists, for it could simply be wishful thinking. But it does show that a God worthy of human worship is one who, by definition, must contain in himself all possible perfections and that, in the non-material realm, this can and does include beauty. This understanding of God does not rely on philosophy alone. It is grounded in God's disclosure of himself, witnessed in the Scriptures, as will be explored more fully later, especially in Chapters 5 and 6.

God is 'beauty so ancient and withal so fresh'.[3] This beauty is therefore inevitably reflected in the universe which he has made. The analogy with an artist and artistic creation is an old and familiar one. A Henry Moore sculpture is immediately recognizable. The massive shapes, the familiar themes like mother and child, the strange yet satisfying relation of parts to each other and to the whole, all say 'Henry Moore'. Into those works Henry Moore put himself and his whole feel for life, as Brancusi did, and Jean Arp and countless others whose works similarly reflect their creators. Experts in ancient sculpture can tell us that a particular Roman statue is a copy of one by Praxiteles, now lost. There is something so distinctive about a statue by him that its character remains, even through endless copies over hundreds of years. So God puts himself unreservedly into his work, as a novelist puts himself into his novel and a dramatist into his play.

An artistic creation exists independently of its maker. So also the universe. God has *created* it, given it a life of its own. The beauty of the world is therefore first of all an aspect of the created order. 'It will flame out, like shining from shook foil',[4] as Hopkins put it in his now well-known line. In the beauty of other people 'Self flashes off frame and face'.[5]

Another analogy, which suggests a closer relationship between divine and created beauty, pictures the relationship between God and the world as akin to that between soul and body. The world is seen as God's body. As a person expresses themselves in a kiss or a handshake, so we might say, the beauty of the world conveys and bodies forth to us the beauty of God. It is better to talk about God *acting* as the soul of the world rather than being the soul of the world. For it is only by utterly transcending the world that he is able to be present in and fill every point of it.[6] But being so transcendent he chooses to fill all things with his presence. Being so intimately present in and through all things, the world becomes a sign and sacrament of his beauty. As that remarkable French religious thinker Simone Weil put it:

> The beauty of the world is Christ's tender smile for us coming through matter. He is really present in the universal beauty. The love of this beauty proceeds from God dwelling in our souls and goes out to God present in the universe. It is also like a sacrament.[7]

Elsewhere, in a vivid image, she compares the universe to the stick of a blind man.[8] Not everyone is able to see the beauty of God in the beauty of the world but we all experience it. As the blind man taps the pavement with his stick, we touch God or rather God touches us through experiences of beauty, whether we are aware of this or not.

The Greek word *kalon*, which we usually translate as 'beautiful', has a much greater breadth in Greek.

It is the right, the fitting, the good, that which is appropriate to a being, that in virtue of which it possesses its integrity, its health, its security; only insofar as it embraces all this, is *kalon* also, by way of confirmation and proof, the beautiful.[9]

Especially telling is the fact that the Greek version of the Hebrew Scriptures, the one used by most of the early Fathers, translates the refrain in the first chapter of Genesis: 'And God saw everything that he had made, and behold, it was very good', as 'behold it was very *kala*'. This brings out a point emphasized by many Christians down the ages, namely that there is an integral connection between all that exists, its goodness and its beauty; so they write of the splendour or radiance of being. The word being refers to all things visible and invisible, the created order on earth, the communion of saints and God himself. All that is, is fundamentally good; so all that is, radiates with the divine splendour. This means that truly to discern the existence of anything, whether a flower or a grain of sand, is to see its finite existence rooted in the ground of being, God himself; it is to discern glimmerings of eternal light, flames or flashes of divine beauty.

Augustine, in his search for truth, questioned all he came across about the goal of his love. He asked the earth and other finite objects what they knew. Each replied that it was not God.

And I said to all these things in my external environment: 'Tell me of my God who you are not, tell me something about him.' And with a great voice they cried out: 'He made us' (Psalm 99.3). My question was the attention I gave to them, and their response was their beauty.

'Surely this beauty should be self-evident to all who are of sound mind', wrote Augustine.

There is no alteration in the voice which is their beauty. If one person sees while another sees and questions, it is not that they appear one way to the first and another to the second. It is rather that the created order speaks to all, but is understood by those who hear its outward voice and compare it with the truth within themselves.[10]

In short, it is the beauty of the created order which gives an answer to our questionings about God. This beauty 'speaks' to us. We attend to the things of the world, our very attention being a question. 'And their response was their beauty.' Their beauty directs us away from them to God our Creator. This is, however, only grasped by those who relate what they see with their eyes to what they think with their minds and judge in their hearts. It is only 'understood by those who hear its outward voice and compare it with the truth within themselves'.

For a Christian the world is good both because God, who is supreme good, has created it and because, in the person of his Son, he has embraced it in a human life. Even more than that, in his Resurrection he has raised earthly beauty to everlasting life. For these reasons the Church has always strongly resisted those distortions of faith which suggest that the physical world, the material order, including its beauty, is evil or inferior in such a way as to be despised. Gnosticism and Manichaeism are just two of the 'isms' that the Church has rejected. Sadly, some of the world-denying strain of Neo-Platonism, as well as the negative view of the material world put forward by Manichaeism, has tainted historic Christianity. Against this we must insist that the Hebraic, Jewish view is the truth of the matter. The physical world, including our bodies, is created fundamentally good and beautiful. The beauty of the world is to be recognized and rejoiced in, affirmed and embraced.

Nevertheless, there is a balance to be kept. Against those who disparage the beauty of this world in the quest for a higher spiritual beauty, the Church insists that earthly beauty is to be enjoyed as the gift of a generous giver. Against those who pursue finite beauty in isolation from other values or its source in the divine beauty, the Christian faith teaches that human beauty can only be properly appreciated and enjoyed when it is seen in the light of and in relation to the divine glory.

A heroic attempt to achieve a right balance can be seen in St Augustine himself. He loved beauty, it was the mainspring of his life. Although, in contrast to many in his time, he admits to not having a highly developed sense of smell, he loved light. As Peter Brown has written:

> Above all, he was surrounded by light. The African sunlight was the 'Queen of all colours pouring down over everything'. He was acutely alive to the effects of light. His only poem is in praise of the warm glow of the Easter candle.

He loved sounds. He loved and was deeply moved by music.

> Augustine's world is full of sounds: the chanting of the psalms, songs at harvest time, and, most delightful of all, the entrancing speech of his fellow men ... 'A speech, imparting its message with charm, well-tuned to touch the feelings of its hearers; the melodious rhythms and high sentiments of a good poem.'[11]

His first book was entitled *On the Beautiful and the Fitting*, a book now unfortunately lost but which sought to draw a distinction between something which is beautiful in itself and that which is beautiful because it is adapted to the whole to which it belongs.

Augustine had a passion for beauty. But he was acutely aware of its dangers. He writes of the pleasures of the ear having a tenacious hold on him and physical light having a seductive and dangerous sweetness. In short, he was conscious of being in 'this immense jungle full of traps and dangers'. Stern spiritual discipline was needed. Yet even this was not enough. Divine beauty itself had to shine upon him. In a famous passage he writes:

> Late have I loved you, beauty so old and so new: Late have I loved you. And see, you were within and I was in the external world and sought you there, and in my unlovely state I plunged into those lovely created things that you made. You were with me, and I was not with you. The lovely things kept me far from you, though if they did not have their existence in you, they had no existence at all. You called and cried out loud and shattered my deafness. You were radiant and resplendent, you put to flight my blindness. You were fragrant, and I drew in my breath and now pant after you. I tasted you, and I feel that hunger and thirst for you. You touched me, and I am set on fire to attain the peace which is yours.[12]

Augustine did not reject the beauty of the world, he moved from a lower to a higher aesthetic. He enjoyed learning, the arts, and beauty. But in his pre-Christian phase he had, he came to think, his back to the source of light.

> I had my back to the light and my face towards the things which are illuminated. So my face, by which I was enabled to see the things lit up, was not itself illuminated.[13]

To use another analogy, he imagines a man giving his betrothed a ring and she saying 'The ring is enough. I do not want to see his face again.' This is a terrible distortion of what should prevail. The gift is to be appreciated but it is the giver who is to be loved.

Another person who sought to get the balance right between created and uncreated beauty was Gerard Manley Hopkins. His love for the beauty of nature needs no underlining for his poems on aspects of the natural world are as widely appreciated as any in the language. But Hopkins also drew and painted. He loved music, especially that of Purcell. He wrote and analysed endlessly about detailed, particular beauties.

Hopkins wrote to Robert Bridges: 'I think no one can admire beauty of the body more than I do', but he went on to say that 'this kind of beauty is dangerous'.[14] There are, he wrote, different kinds of beauty, not only of the body but of the mind and of the character. He then proceeded to outline an Aristotelean rather than a Platonic view of the relationship between physical and spiritual beauty. All beauty of the body, he said, expresses beauty of the soul. Genius is a form of beauty but 'there may be genius uninformed by character'. He gives the example of Tennyson, who had wonderful poetic gifts but whose thoughts were commonplace and wanting in nobility. In contrast, Robert Burns had lesser poetic gifts but a richness and beauty of character which lends worth to some of his smallest fragments. This view is further expounded in a letter to the poet Coventry Patmore in which he discusses how there can be such a thing as beautiful evil. 'Beautiful evil is found, but it is nature's monstrosity.' A beautiful soul will express itself in the finest proportion of feature, insofar as it can assert itself over recalcitrant matter, which it cannot necessarily do perfectly. Evil, however, does not come from nature. 'It comes from wicked will, freedom of choice, abusing the beauty, the good of its nature.'[15] In short, we might come across a person of great beauty of body and cleverness of mind (which is in itself a beauty), but who uses these for cruel ends. The mind and body retain something of the beauty of their being, for being is created good, but the evil will also be evident.

Hopkins has an almost ecstatic delight in all forms of beauty but he knows that what matters above all is that the human will be in harmony with the divine will. This comes out in a number of his poems. An attractive child, who makes a charming answer to him, evokes the verse:

Mannerly-hearted! More than handsome face —
Beauty's bearing or muse of mounting vein,
All, in this case, bathed in high hallowing grace ... [16]

Especially revealing of Hopkins's attitude is his poem 'To what serves Mortal Beauty?' Mortal beauty, he begins, is dangerous, because it sets the blood dancing. But it also does good. It 'keeps warm men's wits to the things that are'. He then gives the example of Gregory, who saw some beautiful fair-haired slaves in the market and was so taken by them he enquired where they came from. He learnt that they came from England and the result was that when he became Pope he sent the mission headed by Augustine (of Canterbury). Gregory did not linger over the physical beauty of the boys. The glimpse of their beauty evoked another love. For we are to love 'men's selves. Self flashes off frame and face.'

What do then? How meet beauty? Merely meet it: own,
Home at heart, heaven's sweet gift; then leave, let that alone.
Yea, wish that though, wish all, God's better beauty, grace. [17]

We are to welcome and delight in created beauty but at the same time acknowledge its source in God and wish for his 'better beauty, grace'. Hopkins gave that creed expression in his poems. For on a number of occasions when he extols the beauty of someone, he ends by praying that they may grow in Christ and be kept safe in eternal life.

One caveat is necessary at this point. To acknowledge the source of earthly beauty in God does not mean that we need to have one eye on earth and another in heaven. As Simone Weil and Dietrich Bonhoeffer both emphasized, we should give ourselves wholly and without thought of anything else to the beautiful, with a single eye. God is implicit when we do this and in so doing we are saved from half-heartedness and semi-attentiveness. In the same way that we want someone who is driving a lorry towards us to be concentrating on what they are doing, this is what God wants of them at that moment, so in attending to the particular person or object before us we are to give our whole attention. As D. H. Lawrence put it in one of his most powerful poems: 'Thought is a man in his wholeness wholly attending.'[18]

Experiences of beauty, whether in nature or in art, are among the most precious and powerful given to us. Beauty has the strange effect of at once beckoning us to itself and pointing beyond itself to that which seems tantalizingly unattainable. It draws us to itself and through itself. Plato, Plotinus, Augustine and many distinguished minds since then have sought to give this phenomenon philosophical expression. They have thought of beauty as an absolute, existing in its own right and making itself felt through all earthly and finite beauty as well as through beautiful souls and spiritual values. If God is the giver of all good gifts and contains within himself all possible perfections, then he must be beauty as much as he is goodness and truth.

For human beings there is always a narrow path to walk between undervaluing earthly beauty in the light of the perfect and eternal beauty of God on the one hand, and so rejoicing in earthly beauty that God is forgotten or rejected. The examples of Augustine and Gerard Manley Hopkins, however, show that it is possible to achieve a balance. Few have been as passionate in their love of beauty as Augustine and Hopkins. Beauty was what haunted, drove and sustained them. Both found their longing for beauty fulfilled in God. Both exulted in the beauties of the world and saw them irradiated by the light of eternal beauty.

There is a spiritual tightrope to walk; there is also an aesthetic one. We can see this by contrasting the approach of a still-life painter when she is in her studio, with that of her prayers in church. Still-life painting, like much poetry, derives its quality from focusing on the particular. The painter is not trying to get behind or beyond the object but attempting to see and depict it in all its unique individuality of colour, shape and texture. Yet kneeling in church, that same painter goes beyond the particular to the universal, beyond the finite to the infinite, the limited to the unlimited. As the use of such words suggests, we are immediately in the realm of abstraction, and abstraction does not always lend itself to art. Yet the attempt to see the particular in all its particularity, and the yearning to go through or beyond the particular to the universal in which it is grounded, are both deeply embedded in the human heart. The special insight of Christianity, as opposed to Platonism, is that the divine beauty is to be seen in and through the particular, of which the Incarnation is the supreme expression. The religious mind aligns itself easily with the universalizing tendency. It was the special genius of Hopkins, drawing on the influence of Duns Scotus, to see the particular and the universal, the human and the divine together. This is one of the features that gives the poetry of Hopkins its creative strength and tension.

Hopkins loved beauty. But he loved truth and goodness no less. This triad of beauty, truth and goodness points to their ground and unifying source in the divine glory.

Notes

1 Plato, *The Symposium* (Penguin, 1951), pp. 92–3.

2 Plotinus, *The Enneads*, i. 6. I (Penguin, 1991), pp. 49, 52.

3 St Augustine, *Confessions* – an old translation of the passage cited already (p. 6).

4 Gerard Manley Hopkins, 'God's Grandeur' in *Poems*, ed. W. H. Gardner and W. H. Mackenzie (OUP, 1970), p. 66.

5 'To what serves Mortal Beauty?' in *Poems*, p. 98.

6 Austin Farrer, *Faith and Speculation* (A. & C. Black, 1967), chapter X, and *A Science of God?* (Bles, 1966), chapter 5.

7 Simone Weil, *Waiting on God* (Fontana, 1959), p. 120.

8 *The Notebooks of Simone Weil*, trans. A. Wills (Routledge & Kegan Paul, 1956), vol. 1, pp. 19, 252.

9 Hans Urs von Balthasar, *The Glory of the Lord*, vol. IV (T. & T. Clark, 1982), p. 201.

10 *Confessions*, pp. 183–4.

11 Peter Brown, *Augustine of Hippo* (Faber, 1967), pp. 35–6.

12 *Confessions*, p. 201.

13 *Confessions*, p. 70.

14 *Gerard Manley Hopkins, Selected Letters*, ed. Catherine Phillips (OUP, 1990), p. 131.

15 *Gerard Manley Hopkins, Selected Letters*, pp. 190ff.

16 'The Handsome Heart' in *Poems*, p. 81.

17 'To what serves Mortal Beauty?' in *Poems*, p. 98.

18 D. H. Lawrence, 'Thought' in *Complete Poems*, ed. Vivian de Sola Pinto and Warren Roberts, vol. II (Heinemann), p. 673.

F O U R

∾∾∾∾∾∾∾∾∾∾∾∾

Divine Glory

The poet W. B. Yeats wrote about a 'Terrible Beauty'.[1] William Blake in describing the numinous, awe-ful quality of a tiger's being wrote of a 'fearful symmetry'.[2] These paradoxical phrases bring out the point, already referred to in Chapter 2, that beauty is very different from mere prettiness. In some contexts the word beauty, by itself, seems too weak to convey the powerful impact a work of art or scene in nature has made on us. An accomplished performance of *King Lear* will have clear elements of beauty about it but something in addition to beauty will be conveyed. It will disclose profound truth; bring home the inescapable moral dimension to life. *King Lear* encompasses suffering and tragedy. So do many works of art, the paintings of Goya and the Passion music of Bach to give just two examples.

At its least adequate the word beauty is close to conveying the notion of what is only decorative. This is a fine feature, not to be disparaged in its proper place. But there is also the searing, disturbing, haunting element which is present in many of the greatest works of art. For this reason Patrick Sherry rejects the objective analysis of beauty argued for earlier.[3] For him this is too formal. He places more emphasis on the terribleness of beauty as well as on the strong subjective feelings aroused by such experiences, which he includes in his definition of it. For the sake of clarity I prefer a different approach. Beauty, properly understood, needs to be seen in conjunction with truth and goodness. It is because beauty is, quite properly, associated with these other qualities that it can sometimes seem wracking and awesome.

Paul Tillich was another person who believed that the word beauty has become so associated with what is pretty that a substitute for it needs to be found. He preferred to talk about the expressive power of works of art. According to him every work of art expresses some aspect of reality and it is this which gives art its universal meaning and power.[4] Like Tillich I believe that genuine art catches, conveys and participates in some aspect of reality, even ultimate reality, to use his phrase. This is the truth content of art, which Tillich also refers to as its depths or import. There is, however, also the form, without which no work of art would exist and which is also included in Tillich's analysis. Beauty has to do with this form. To be beautiful as opposed to merely pretty, it needs to be associated with other values like truth or integrity. But the two values of beauty and truth are distinct, if in the end inseparable. It muddies the water to subsume one into the other.

Constable wrote that there are two faults to be avoided in painting: one is 'the absurdity of imitation' and the other is 'bravura', which he defined as 'going beyond the truth'. It is the truth of a landscape that the artist is trying to get at. This means avoiding all copying, either of other works of art or of what is before the eyes, as though a photograph is being produced. It also means opening the eyes to try to see what is actually there, without imposing our own illusions and fantasies on it. Sometimes, in order to sell his pictures, Constable put in a little of what he called 'eye salve'. But he was well aware of what he was doing and that this was a departure from the highest

48

standards of artistic integrity which he set himself. In 1826 he painted his famous landscape *The Cornfield*. It shows a lane leading to a cornfield, the wind blowing in the sky, the trees and the corn. Also in the picture are a sheepdog, sheep and a boy picking a flower. 'I do hope to sell this present picture — as it has certainly got a little more eye salve than I usually condescend to give them.'[5]

All forms of art are in the business of truth: truth of eye and ear and mind. True beauty is inseparable from the quest for truth. When the attempt to produce something beautiful is separated from truth the result is sentimentality.

It is well known that Rembrandt went through a series of crises in his life, personal and financial, as a result of which his art radically changed in character. This is particularly noticeable in the way that he switched from grandiose descriptions of biblical scenes to ones in which Jesus is depicted in a much more human, lowly manner.

Rembrandt finally turned his back on the glorification of man which had become the classical ideal, and which reached its zenith in Baroque art. Thus he shows us that he has learned that it is a humble thing to be a man. From this time the beautiful ceased to be an end in itself for him. He realized that beauty must serve something higher, namely truth, or else it is in danger of becoming an empty shell, falsifying the reality of life. If beauty accepts this part, it acquires a new substance through which the eternal shines.[6]

The attempt to get at the truth of things in this way is inseparable from certain moral qualities. Artistic integrity is the most obvious quality that is required. Here we come across the fact that sometimes an artist may be all over the place in their personal life whilst still producing works of great quality. This is because, whatever the mess in the rest of their life, they are still totally committed to their work, brooking no compromises.

Patrick White describes such an artist in his novel *The Vivisector*.[7] The artist's moral life is totally at sea. But he is haunted by a vision that he strives and strives to produce on canvas. He is totally serious about this; utterly given over to the task.

Hopkins once wrote to Robert Bridges to say that 'A kind of touchstone of the highest or most living art is seriousness; not gravity but the being in earnest with your subject — reality'.[8] He then went on to remark that some of the most famous works of art are not really in earnest and he instanced Roman literature. One of the reasons that the philosopher Ludwig Wittgenstein fell out with Bertrand Russell was that Wittgenstein felt Russell was not fundamentally serious, even about mathematical logic.[9] Such fierce integrity is usually very difficult to live with.

One of the problems of bringing morality into a discussion of beauty or art is that the word sets up such misleading associations. People immediately tend to think that sex or violence is being referred to. But all works of art inevitably express a feeling for life and convey certain moral values. There is no morally neutral realm in art or elsewhere. Nothing in this life is value-free. And some works of art which are bitterly attacked as being immoral are in fact the product of a profoundly moral view of existence.

Another quality that is necessary for great art is love. Truth without love leads in the end to bitterness and cynicism. An artist who is always disdainful, who can only see the worst, who hates what they are working on, cannot produce great art. Love means, first, an act of self-transcendence, in order to see truly what is being depicted whether in words or paint or stone or any other medium. Secondly, the artist needs a sense of the value of what is portrayed. The person depicted might be truly awful, even utterly cruel but, unless they are to be a cardboard cutout or a piece of propaganda, it will be necessary even so to retain a sense of the pity and tragedy of their life. *Sunt lacrimae rerum*, as the Roman poet Virgil put it: 'There are tears in things.' Art needs all that Simone Weil meant by 'attention'. And attention, she argued, means putting aside the illusion that 'my eye' is the centre of the world and focusing on things as they are. To focus on things as they are, in this way, is to share in God's act of self-renunciation, his love.

Stanley Spencer once said:

When I have reached a certain degree of awareness of the 'Touch-me-not' quality of things I am filled with a desire to establish this thing revealing quite clearly this quality. Love is the essential power in the creation of art, and love is not a talent ... It establishes, once and for all time, the final and perfect identity of every created thing.[10]

We can see the obverse of this truth in some of Stanley Spencer's own work and its relation to the circumstances of his life at the time. His paintings of Patricia Preece, though painted with extraordinary clarity and precision, strike many as disturbing, with a nauseating rather than an exhilarating disturbance. Stanley Spencer became obsessed with Patricia Preece and his marriage to Hilda, whom he never ceased to love, broke up. Patricia Preece was a lesbian — their marriage was never consummated — who married him for his money and mocked him ruthlessly. The portraits of Patricia Preece are technically brilliant but they repel rather than attract because they reflect Spencer's convoluted feelings at this time.

The relationship between moral truth and beauty is a puzzling one. But they cannot in the end be separated. This comes out very clearly in the feelings of some war photographers to their work. In a television programme, *Stains of War*, the photographer George Roger spoke about his visit to Belsen after the war and his professional work, arranging 'beautiful compositions' of the dead. Approached by a prisoner who tried to talk to him but fell dead at his feet from weakness, Roger was positioning himself for a good angle on the corpse when he suddenly thought: 'My God, what's happened to me?' He never undertook military assignments again. All the photographers who took part in the programme felt that their work had coarsened their feelings. Larry Burrows, famous for his images from Vietnam, wondered 'whether it was right to capitalize on the grief of others'. Fouad Khoury, working in the Lebanon, found an editor's demand 'Don't you have any carbonized heads on the pavement?' too much, and gave it up.[11]

The photographers felt there was an irreconcilable clash between aesthetic considerations and decent human feelings, between arousing interest in the readers of magazines and newspapers and proper feelings of shock and revulsion. Yet war photographers, like doctors, have a job to do. They need to keep the public informed of what is happening. Sometimes, as in the case of photographs from the Vietnam War, they play a vital role in arousing the revulsion and opposition of people at home to the war. Yet if the pictures are too shocking and revolting readers will not be pleased and magazine editors will not in the end publish them. People like to feel a mild sense of outrage or pity. So the pictures inevitably have a beautifying element to them, which makes them acceptable. They report the brutal truth but not in too brutal a way. There is a dilemma here which does not lend itself to simplistic solutions.

The question of the relationship between beauty, brutal truth and politics is raised particularly acutely in the case of Wilhelm Furtwängler (1886-1955), who was, alongside Toscanini, the most widely revered conductor of his time. Furtwängler stayed in Germany as an esteemed conductor all through the Nazi period. He has been bitterly attacked and also defended for this. Some have argued, for example, that he did at a personal level try to save some Jews. The truth seems to be that whilst he was not a rabid anti-Semite, he shared the general anti-Semitism of conservative nationalists of his type. Furthermore, his very presence in Germany at that time, still able to operate as a distinguished conductor, gave a gloss of respectability to the regime. As Bruno Walter told Furtwängler after the war, he had to consider the fact that

> Your art was used as a conspicuously effective means of propaganda for the regime of the devil ... that the presence and performance of an artist of your stature abetted every horrible crime against culture and morality, or at least, gave considerable support to them ... In the light of all that, of what significance is your assistance in the isolated cases of a few Jews?

Furtwängler defended himself, both during and after the Third Reich, against such critics by maintaining that his overriding purpose had been to keep spiritual and human values alive in a regime that had consistently tried to destroy them. 'Human beings', he told Toscanini, 'are free wherever Wagner and Beethoven are played ... music transports them to regions where the Gestapo can do them no harm.' After the war he told the de-Nazification hearing that his aim had been nothing less than 'the maintenance of liberty, humanity and justice in human life'.[12] Everything he had done, including the minor compromises, had been for the sake of higher artistic values.

Furtwängler's view of music is not unlike certain views of religion: it is apart from the political sphere, able to give solace and consolation in the most terrible times. Yet Furtwängler's case brings out clearly that such a view of art is inadequate. It cannot be separated in this way from the wider claims of human feeling and political commitment. It might have been different if Furtwängler was making his music to sustain the inmates of Belsen in their last hours or even if he had fled Germany and made his music in Britain to support and inspire the struggle against the Nazis. But his music gave consolation to those who should not have been consoled, transported the Gestapo (as well as the victims of the Gestapo) to regions where they no longer had to face what they ought to have faced, the terrible cruelty that they were perpetuating. In saying that he was not a politician, only a musician, Furtwängler allowed himself to be used politically. This is not to say that art need always be political or that the political context must always be taken into account. It is however to say that art cannot be totally disassociated from wider considerations. In the struggle against apartheid in South Africa, for example, there was all the world of difference between a black choir bringing delight to the people of a township, giving them some enjoyment in their harsh struggle, and a visiting choir from Europe, whose visit could be used by the apartheid regime to give an air of normality and respectability to what was going on.

When goodness, truth and beauty are combined we have glory. When boundless goodness, total truth and sublime beauty are combined in supreme degree, we have divine glory. The word glory has come to mean honour and renown. In church we often repeat the *Gloria*: 'Glory to the Father and to the Son and to the Holy Spirit.' But the ascription of glory to God should be seen as a response to the glory that is inherent in his being. Before our recognition and praise, God is in himself all glory in a sublime conjunction of beauty, truth and love. This glory is majestic. It brings wonder and awe and worship.

The divine glory was disclosed first of all to the people of Israel. In the Hebrew Scriptures the word glory and its cognates glorious, glorify, etc. are used many times in relation to God. The glory of God shines out in the beauty and order of creation. 'The heavens declare the glory of God' (Psalm 19.1). This all-glorious God sometimes gives a glimpse of his glory to particular people. When Moses received the Ten Commandments on Mount Horeb, he was both in awe and as one speaking to God as a friend: 'The skin of his face shone because he had been talking with God' (Exodus 34.29). Sometimes in the Scriptures God is depicted as one who makes himself known by his superior power, his sheer might. He can do what other gods cannot do and break the bodies as well as the wills of

The Baptism of Christ _by Piero della Francesca. National Gallery._

The Old Testament Trinity by Andrei Rublev. Andrei Rublev Museum, Moscow. Photo SVS Press

recalcitrant people. This would be intolerable tyranny except that it was linked to his loving kindness, his undeviating goodwill towards his people and the luminous beauty of his holiness. What stops the God of Israel being experienced as sheer terror is his being as love and beauty. He is not just power but glory. Power can browbeat us but glory lures and entices us by stirring what we most deeply desire.

The divine glory is experienced in worship: 'Then the cloud covered the tent of meeting, and the glory of the Lord filled the tabernacle' (Exodus 40.34). Above all, God is present with his people in all their wanderings and trials. 'For throughout all their journeys the cloud of the Lord was upon the tabernacle by day, and fire was in it by night, in the sight of all the house of Israel' (Exodus 40.38).

It is the Christian conviction that this glory is fully known in Jesus Christ. He is 'the Lord of glory' (1 Corinthians 2.8). The glory of God in Jesus Christ is a theme that runs throughout the New Testament. 'He reflects the glory of God and bears the very stamp of his nature' (Hebrews 1.3). But it is in John's Gospel where the theme receives most sustained and consistent treatment. When the Word became flesh, 'We beheld his glory, glory as of the only Son from the Father' (John 1.14). This glory was revealed in the signs, starting at Cana of Galilee (John 2.11). Above all, however, the glory of God shines out in the Cross and Resurrection. Jesus prays that in his life and the coming climax of his death God might be glorified. But this glorification of the Father is also a glorification of the Son. For Jesus has given himself over totally to do his Father's will. His Father's work is what he came to accomplish. Because his being is one with the Father, through all temptations and suffering, it is his glory that is revealed as well as that of the Father (John 12.27-33; 17.1-5). John looks at Jesus through the eyes of one who believes in him; in the light of the Resurrection and coming of the Spirit. He had come 'to see' and believe.

The picture painted by Mark's Gospel is very different. It

stresses the failure of the disciples, the betrayal by Judas, the denial by Peter and the abandonment by the disciples. Everyone falls away and in the end Jesus is left on the Cross uttering the agonized words 'My God, my God, why hast thou forsaken me?' (Mark 15.34). The glory of God in Christ, except at the Transfiguration, is hidden.

In Mark and John we have the two poles of Christian truth. To generalize the truth revealed in Christ, God's glory is revealed in humble, self-effacing lives of faith and love. It can be fully present in failure and ignominy. It is almost entirely a glory that is veiled. Yet, however hidden, lives of sacrificial love lived in response to the Father manifest the glory of God and the glory of Christ. For Christ has been raised and his Spirit is with us, unveiling Christ's journey to the Cross as a movement to the Father and revealing the divine glory. In the light of this many of our standard notions of success and failure are radically reversed. Christ, the King of Glory, reigns from the tree.

Paul Evdokimov complains that Western art of the Crucifixion depicts Jesus as defeated and abandoned.[13] In contrast, the icons of the Orthodox Church never lose sight of the triumph of God's loving purpose in him. But the difference between Eastern and Western art at this point is simply the difference between a Markan and a Johannine perspective. The Church is always faced with a challenge: how to depict, whether in art or words, the brutal reality of the Crucifixion without leaving the impression that it is just one more gratuitous act of violence in a world of violence. And how to depict the Resurrection without giving the impression that it is simply a happy ending tacked on at the end, cheapening the travail that has gone before.[14] There is a sense in which the Resurrection does reverse the human verdict of the Cross. Yet, at a more profound level, it simply reveals the divine love poured out there.

Christ reveals the divine glory because he is the truth of God and the love of God, in human terms. But what about the beauty of God? Gerard Manley Hopkins said in a sermon: 'There met in

Jesus Christ all things that can make man lovely and lovable. In his body he was most beautiful.' He then goes on to quote what he believes to be an early description of Jesus:

Moderately tall, well-built and slender in frame, his features straight and beautiful, his hair inclining to auburn, parted in the midst, curling and clustering about the ears and neck as the leaves of a filbert, so to speak, upon the nut. He wore also a forked beard and this as well as the locks upon his head were never touched by a razor or shears.

He argues for Christ's physical beauty from Luke 2.52, and from his birth by special work of the Holy Ghost.

I leave it to you, brethren, to picture him, in whom the fullness of the Godhead dwelt bodily, in his bearing how majestic, how strong and yet how lovely and lissome in his limbs, in his look how earnest, grave but kind.

He then goes on to contrast this physical beauty with how Jesus looked at the Crucifixion:

In his passion all this strength was spent, this lissomeness crippled, this beauty wrecked, this majesty beaten down.[15]

Earlier writers fight shy of extolling Christ's physical beauty, indeed there is discussion about whether we should think only of his spiritual beauty or of both spiritual and physical beauty. All writers, however, are agreed in applying the words of Isaiah 53.2 to Christ on the Cross: 'He had no form or comeliness that we should look at him, and no beauty that we should desire him.' For our sake the beauty of God takes on ugliness. As Augustine put it in a sermon: 'His deformity is our beauty.'

In his description of the physical build of Christ, Gerard Manley Hopkins is in grave danger of slipping into kitsch.

Kitsch is the enemy of all that is true, good and beautiful. In his novel *The Unbearable Lightness of Being*, Milan Kundera has a remarkable chapter on kitsch which he defines as 'the absolute denial of shit, in both the literal and the figurative senses of the word; Kitsch excludes everything from its purview which is essentially unacceptable in human existence.'[16] What is important about Kundera's novel is that he sees the inescapable connection between art, morality and metaphysics. In art kitsch takes the form of the pretty, the sentimental and fashionable. It excludes all that is truly disturbing and harrowing. In morality kitsch takes the form of totalitarianism, the exclusion of all that is individual and distinctive. Kundera's particular focus is Communism. What repels one of Kundera's characters is 'not nearly so much the ugliness of the Communist world ... as the mask of beauty it tried to wear – in other words, Communist Kitsch. The model of Communist Kitsch is a ceremony called May Day.' During May Day parades there is feigned enthusiasm, neat colourful clothing, brass bands, dazzling smiles, in short 'proper *agreement*'. Yet kitsch is no less present in capitalist societies. Sabina, Kundera's character, gets taken for a drive in an American Senator's car. He sees some children and starts to wax sentimental.

> Kitsch causes two tears to flow in quick succession. The first tear says: How nice to see the children running on the grass! The second tear says: How nice to be moved, together with all mankind, by children running on the grass! It is the second tear that makes Kitsch Kitsch. The brotherhood of man on earth will be possible only on a base of Kitsch.

By the last sentence he means that only an illusory, sentimental and in the end cruel denial of the fundamental differences between human beings will bring about what Communism thinks of as the brotherhood of man. But not only Communists. Whenever politicians rush to kiss children in front of cameras the same tendency is at work. 'Kitsch is the aesthetic ideal of all politicians and all political parties and movements.' It leads to concentration camps and the Gulag. 'The gulag is a septic tank used by totalitarian Kitsch to dispose of its refuse.'

Kundera thinks that the attitude which produces artistic and political kitsch has its origins in a particular metaphysic. This metaphysic denies reality as it is, tries to pretend that what disgusts or excites us does not really do so. He does, I think, muddle his argument at this point by describing these attempts to deny reality as a kind of faith, 'a categorical agreement with being', and he links it to the Genesis story in which it is said that everything that God created is good. Disgust and sexual excitement only emerge, according to some theologians, after human beings have been expelled from Paradise. But Christians, together with Jews and Muslims, wish to affirm the fundamental goodness of created existence without in any way denying the horrors it now contains. Those horrors have to be acknowledged as such without any attempt to minimize or gloss them over. One of the strengths of Kundera is that like Camus, and Ivan Karamazov in Dostoevsky's novel, he keeps alive the sense of protest against the world as it exists at the moment. Christians are sometimes prone to a premature acceptance of things as they are, when God is calling us to protest against things as they are. The categorical agreement with being in which Christians have faith is first of all in God himself, the ground of our being. Secondly, in the innocence of creation as it springs from God and thirdly, in an ultimate resolution of life's contradictions. Between primeval innocence and that ultimate state when God will be all in all, protest against the way things are is not just an optional extra, it is a moral necessity. This questioning, doubting, protesting can co-exist with and lead into a profound faith, as it did for Job.

It was argued earlier that all art involves form. However horrendous the truths to be depicted, whether in a poem, a novel, on the stage or in a picture, art cannot escape from some degree of shaping and patterning. This inevitably beautifies what in the raw evokes only sheer revulsion, disgust, horror. And this sets up a problem. For is it morally right to beautify, in any way at all, what quite properly revolts us morally, spiritually or aesthetically? This is a question which is pursued further in the last chapter. The two points I wish to make here are that first, kitsch, in whatever form, is an enemy of the Christian faith and must be exposed as such. Secondly, kitsch reveals to us that the aesthetic, the moral and the spiritual realms are inseparably interconnected. The failure of kitsch is a moral and spiritual failure as much as an aesthetic one. The success of a work of art is a moral and spiritual success as much as it is an aesthetic triumph. The beauty of Christ is not a sentimental prettiness, however much nineteenth-century kitsch religious souvenirs have shaped people to think of him in that way. We do not know the extent of Christ's physical beauty. We do, however, in faith, believe that there is in him a spiritual loveliness which permeates his whole being, breaks down our resistance and wins us to him.

William Golding's most ambitious and perhaps least under-stood novel, *Darkness Visible*, has as its central character a strange man called Matty. Matty emerges on the first page of the book out of the heart of a devastating fire in London's dockland during the Blitz. He is terribly burned and though the hospital saves his life he remains grotesquely disfigured. One side of his face is hardly there, an ear is shrivelled up and only a flap of hair is left on his head. He can hardly get words out of his mouth. The dominant feature of Matty's life is his rejection by others. Yet he exists for a purpose and part of the purpose is the redemption of a pederast who, like other people, is physically repelled by Matty. Matty is blown up in an explosion but after his death the pederast Mr Pedigree has a vision of Matty:

He came slowly to Mr Pedigree who found his approach not only natural but even agreeable for the boy was not really as awful to look at as one might think, there where he waded along waist deep in gold. He came and stood before Pedigree and looked down at him. Pedigree understood that they were in a park of mutuality and closeness where the sunlight lay right on the skin. 'You know it was all your fault Matty.' Matty seemed to agree; and really the boy was quite pleasant to look at![17]

Matty could not be uglier, with an ugliness brought about by the wickedness of the world. His life is insignificant. Yet Golding wishes to present him as having a spiritual beauty, a spiritual beauty which in the final vision takes the form of physical beauty. The beauty of Christ and of those whose lives are hid with Christ in God, may be opaque. But in the light of the Resurrection it is resplendent.

In a fine sermon on 1 John 4.17-21 St Augustine says that it is by loving that we are made beautiful. By loving us, even when we are ugly, God arouses our love and makes us beautiful.

> But our soul, my brethren, is unlovely by reason of iniquity: by loving God it becomes lovely. What a love must that be that makes the lover beautiful! But God is always lovely, never unlovely, never changeable. Who is always lovely first loved us; and what were we when he loved us but foul and unlovely? But not to leave us foul; but to change us, and of unlovely make us lovely. How shall we become lovely? By loving him who is always lovely. As the love increases in Thee, so the loveliness increases.

Augustine goes on to quote various texts which point to the beauty of Jesus. But he also quotes Isaiah 53: How can Christ be both beauteous and without beauty? He is beautiful with all the beauty of God but

'We saw him, and he had no form nor comeliness' — he made

himself of no reputation, taking upon him the form of a servant, made in the likeness of men, and in fashion found as man. 'He has no form nor comeliness', that he might give thee form and comeliness. What form? What comeliness? The love which is in charity: that loving, thou mayest run; running, mayest love. Thou art fair now.[18]

True beauty is inseparable from the quest for truth and those moral qualities which make for a true quest. In the world of art this means integrity, a refusal to go for easy popularity, for cheap truth; the willingness to transcend the clamant ego, to attend to what is there, in its own terms, however painful. This is why works of art, in whatever medium, as well as having a form which pleases will convey truth which may disturb. The conjunction of beauty with truth and goodness has its origin in God and is what we mean by his glory.

The Bible does not dwell long on beauty in isolation but it has much to say on the subject of glory. The God who is revealed is a God of glory and his glory is destined to illuminate and shine in us. For a Christian this glory is above all revealed in Jesus Christ. This was, for the most part, hidden glory. Only at the Transfiguration and in the light of his Resurrection is Christ's life of self-offering to the Father revealed in all its splendour as the life of God made Man and the destiny of humanity to become like God.

This means that as human beings we will always stand in a profound, puzzling, tensionful relationship to all forms of human beauty. For the full glory of the world about us will be largely hidden in lives of secret self-sacrifice, of unceasing inner prayer, of profound artistic achievement that goes unrecognized in its own time. On the other hand, all that is fine and flourishing, all that is beautiful and radiant as God intends it to be, has its place in that transformed world which belongs first and foremost and finally to the poor and humble.

Notes

1 W. B. Yeats, 'Easter 1916'.

2 William Blake, 'The Tyger'.

3 Patrick Sherry, *Spirit and Beauty* (OUP, 1992), p. 34.

4 Paul Tillich, *On Art and Architecture*, ed. John and Jane Dillenberger (Crossroad, New York, 1987), p. 207.

5 *John Constable's Correspondence*, ed. R. B. Beckett, vol. 6 (Suffolk Records Society, 1969), p. 217.

6 W. A. Visser 't Hooft, *Rembrandt and the Gospel* (SCM, 1957), p. 13.

7 Patrick White, *The Vivisector* (Penguin, 1973).

8 *Gerard Manley Hopkins, Selected Letters*, ed. Catherine Phillips (OUP, 1990), p. 225.

9 Ray Monk, *Ludwig Wittgenstein* (Vintage, 1991), p. 214.

10 Stanley Spencer, *Sermons by Artists* (Golden Cockerel Press, 1934).

11 David Johnson, *Church Times* (13 November 1992).

12 Richard Evans, *The Times Literary Supplement* (13 November 1992).

13 Paul Evdokimov, *The Art of the Icon: A Theology of Beauty* (Oakwood, California, 1990).

14 I have tried to address this problem in *Christ Is Risen* (Mowbray, 1988), chapter 6. See also my essay 'The Resurrection in Some Modern Novels' in *If Christ Be Not Risen*, ed. John Greenhalgh and Elizabeth Russell (Collins, USA, 1988).

15 Gerard Manley Hopkins, *Poems and Prose* (Penguin, 1953), pp. 136ff.

16 Milan Kundera, *The Unbearable Lightness of Being* (Faber, 1985), pp. 243ff.

17 William Golding, *Darkness Visible* (Faber, 1979), p. 265.

18 St Augustine, Homily IX in *The Nicene and Post-Nicene Fathers*, vol. VII (Eerdman, 1983), p. 518.

F I V E

∽∾∽∾∽∾∽∾∽∾∽∾

Eternal Wisdom

P eople associate the Hebrew Scriptures with law and prophetic moral teaching. But they contain another category of religious writings: wisdom literature. The Book of Proverbs, Ecclesiastes and Job are part of this genre. Some of the books of the Apocrypha also belong to this category. The Apocryphal writings formed part of the Bible of the early Church and they are still included in the canonical writings of the Roman Catholic and Orthodox Churches. Unfortunately the Protestant reformers put them in a special category and this has resulted in their comparative neglect.

These writings meant an enormous amount to the early Church. It seems likely that Jesus himself drew on the tradition of wisdom literature much more than is usually recognized. Certainly his ethical teaching is best understood against this background.[1] When it came to interpreting Christ, the concept of eternal wisdom was a key concept both for New Testament and later writers. The writings of Chrysostom and St Augustine in the fourth century are suffused with the spirit of the wisdom writings and studded with quotations from them. The Book of Ecclesiasticus in the Apocrypha, for example, is the most quoted of all the books of Scripture in the first centuries of the Christian era. The great church that the Emperor Justinian had built in Constantinople in the sixth century, still standing as one of the wonders of the world, is dedicated to Holy Wisdom (*Hagia Sophia*).

The concept of God as eternal wisdom is central to my theme for three reasons. First, wisdom is, according to the Scriptures, beautiful; secondly, because the marks of this beauty are proportion and measure, harmony and wholeness; and thirdly, because moral wisdom is integrally linked to these characteristics of beauty and order. In short, the characteristics of wisdom are akin to those of divine glory, considered as a sublime conjunction of beauty, truth and goodness as sketched out in the preceding chapter. The difference is this: in divine glory it is the majestic splendour of God's love, truth and beauty that is set forth. With eternal wisdom it is the ordered beauty of the universe and the ordered beauty of our lives when they are lived at one with the divine purpose for them, that is seen.

First, the beauty of wisdom. In the Wisdom of Solomon, another Apocryphal book, wisdom is described in these words:

For she is a breath of the power of God,
and a pure emanation of the glory of the Almighty;
Therefore nothing defiled gains entrance into her.
For she is a reflection of eternal light,
a spotless mirror of the working of God,
and an image of his goodness.
Though she is but one, she can do all things,
and while remaining in herself, she renews all things;
in every generation she passes into holy souls
and makes them friends of God, and prophets;
for God loves nothing so much as the man who lives with
wisdom.

For she is more beautiful than the sun,
and excels every constellation of the stars.
Compared with the light she is found to be superior,
for it is succeeded by the night,
but against wisdom evil does not prevail.
She reaches mightily from one end of the earth to the
    other,
and she orders all things well.
I loved her and sought her from my youth,
and I desired to take her for my bride,
and I became enamoured of her beauty.
(Wisdom of Solomon 7.25–8.2)

This wonderful passage hardly needs any comment. But we notice that the relationship between wisdom and God is akin to that between the word and God as described in the prologue of John's Gospel; that the beauty of wisdom is such that we are 'enamoured of her beauty' and that her work is that of 'ordering' both the universe and our lives.

This leads on to the second characteristic of wisdom. As that passage put it 'She reaches mightily from one end of the earth to the other, and she orders all things well'. As argued in Chapter 2, form is basic to all beauty: balance, proportion, pattern, all that we mean by wholeness and harmony. In the beginning there was chaos: 'The earth was without form and void' (Genesis 1.2). But the Spirit of God breathed on this formlessness and gave the universe shape, indeed strictly speaking creation and the structures of creation are inseparable. So it is that when we look at a crystal or a leaf we are captivated and awestruck by the patterns we discern. At every point in the universe such patterns can be seen: at the sub-atomic level, in atoms, molecules, cells and multi-cellular structures; in the microcosm and in the macrocosm we see wonder of form. Indeed we can only grasp intellectually what is there by depicting the unimaginable complexity of the material world in forms, at the most basic level in mathematical forms. These structures and patterns of the universe reflect the work of the eternal wisdom. Speaking to wisdom, the writer of the Wisdom of Solomon continues: 'Thou hast arranged all things by measure and number and weight' (11.20). Mediaeval writers took this text and theme to be aesthetic as well as scientific and related both dimensions to the goodness of all that exists. The amazing variety and beauty of creation, held together beneath its multiple forms by an underlying unity, never ceased to make them marvel. As Umberto Eco puts it:

> There was not a single mediaeval writer who did not turn to this theme of the polyphony of the universe; and we find often enough that along with the calm and control of philosophical language there sounded a cry of ecstatic joy: 'when you consider the order and magnificence of the universe ... you will find it to be like a most beautiful canticle ... and the wondrous variety of its creatures to be a symphony of joy and harmony to very excess' (William of Auvergne, *De Anima*, V, 18).[2]

Quite a number of concepts were constructed in order to give philosophical expression to this aesthetic vision of the universe. But they all derived ultimately from the triad of terms given in the Book of Wisdom: number (*numerus*), weight (*pondus*), and measure (*mensura*).

Amongst modern writers it is Simone Weil who assumes the closest connection between order and beauty. Indeed, sometimes, she seems almost to equate the two. When discussing beauty as a form of the implicit love of God she heads the section: 'Love of the Order of the World'.[3] Elsewhere she writes: 'The subject of science is the beautiful (that is to say order, proportion, harmony) in so far as it is suprasensible and necessary.'[4]

The third characteristic of eternal wisdom is the way our

lives, when truly ordered, share in and reflect this wisdom. One of the unfortunate characteristics of the modern world is the way we have split asunder thinking, feeling and morality. Beauty is too often thought of simply in terms of an emotional response. Conscience is usually understood to be a feeling of guilt whilst pure hard thinking is reserved for science. In contrast to this rendering apart of feeling, thinking and morality, our Christian forebears had a unified vision in which mental processes always had a role to play and beauty was an aspect of objective reality. This is in no way meant to denigrate feeling. Mediaeval people felt just as strongly, if not more so, than we do. Nor is this to undervalue any light that psychology might throw on the judgements we make. But we have been created by God with minds. Conscience, for Thomas Aquinas, is a matter not of feeling, but of rational judgement; it is the mind making moral decisions. It is a matter of thinking hard about what in any circumstance is the right course of action in the light of fundamental Christian principles. One of the characteristic features of all wisdom literature is the conviction that right action in the eyes of God is an essentially rational activity. It is sensible to act justly because that will lead to the well-being of oneself as well as of other people. At its worst this kind of moral teaching can seem simply prudential, doing good in order to prosper; or it can come across as banal or simply untrue. Good behaviour does not automatically lead to prosperity all round. But the vital element in this tradition is the conviction that God wants his world to flourish, and he has given us minds to enter into his divine purpose. We can use our minds to grasp his wisdom. In so ordering our lives aright we will reflect the divine wisdom, and in this we will also discern something of the divine beauty.

The unity of beauty, right ordering and moral wisdom is well seen in the work of the sixth-century philosopher Boethius, who influenced many Christian writers in the Middle Ages, especially Dante. Boethius wrote:

In regular harmony
The world moves through its changes;
Seas in competition with each other
Are held in balance by eternal laws;
Phoebus brings rosy dawns
In his golden chariot
That his sister Phoebe may rule the nights
That Hesperus brings;
The ways of the greedy sea
Are kept within fixed bounds,
Nor may the land move out
And extend its limits.
What binds all things to order,
Governing earth and sea and sky,
Is love.
If love's reins slackened
All things held now by mutual love
At once would fall to warring with each other
Striving to wreck that engine of the world
Which now they drive
In mutual trust with motion beautiful.
And love joins peoples too
By a sacred bond,
And ties the knot of holy matrimony
That binds chaste lovers,
Joins too with its law
All faithful comrades.
O happy race of men,
If the love that rules the stars
May also rule your hearts![5]

In this vision the order of the universe, the rhythm of the natural world, is an expression of love. That love is also to be expressed in the ordered beauty of our lives.

The words from William of Auvergne, quoted above by

Umberto Eco, show how easily people then thought of the order of the universe as a kind of music. This view does not belong only to the past. The mathematical models devised to map the foundation of the universe have a beauty about them which is akin to music. The young Ludwig Wittgenstein praised Bertrand Russell's work in such terms: 'He spoke with great feeling about the beauty of *Principia*, and said — what was the highest praise he could give it — that it was like music.'[6] And the relationship between music and spiritual reality has often been suggested.

Cultural anthropologists argue that the origin of all non-visual arts — music, dance, poetry and drama, for example — is to be found in the rhythmic clapping of hands or beating of drums. This is the earliest form of art: simple beat, rhythm, repetition. From this music comes dance, when bodies begin to move to the rhythm; poetry, as words are recited to it; and theatre, which was originally poetic drama. It was easy for people to make the jump from this earthly rhythm to the music of the universe, to which we should be moving in harmony. Both Boethius and Augustine wrote books on music and found in nature an echo of the divine music. Gustav Holst in 'The Hymn to Jesus' set some remarkable words from the Gnostic Gospel of Thomas to music:

Divine grace is dancing.
Fain would I pipe for you: dance ye all. Amen.
Fain would I lament: mourn ye all. Amen.
The heavenly spheres make music for us: Amen.
The holy twelve dance with us.
All things join in the dance.

Ye who dance not, know not what we are knowing. Amen.

Give ye heed unto my dancing:
In me who speak behold yourselves: Amen.
And beholding what I do keep silence on my mysteries.
Divine ye in dancing what I shall do.

71

Until the Renaissance, and even long after, the majority of people thought that the heavenly spheres literally emitted music. We do not think like that. But the mind reflecting on the universe can still open the ear of reason to hear, the mouth to praise and our being to dance. Writing in the eighteenth century Joseph Addison, in a famous hymn, reflects on the cycle of nature. He still believed that

> The spacious firmament on high,
> With all the blue ethereal sky,
> And spangled heavens, a shining frame,
> Their great original proclaim.

Although we cannot hear any music with our ears we can with our minds.

> What though in solemn silence all
> Move round the dark terrestrial ball;
> What though nor real voice nor sound
> Amid their radiant orbs be found;
>
> In reason's ear they all rejoice,
> And utter forth a glorious voice;
> For ever singing as they shine,
> 'The hand that made us is divine.'

Although we do not literally hear music we can attune to the miraculous ordering of the universe with our minds. We see moving patterns of energy, from electrons to galaxies; all things move in measure to the divine music. This is one of the sub-themes of T. S. Eliot's *Four Quartets*. The community dances to the rhythm of the seasons, all things move in measure; and at the mystical timeless moment 'the darkness shall be the light and the stillness the dancing'.[7]

The concept of the word (*logos* in Greek) in the prologue of

St John's Gospel has a rich background. The *logos* was one of the leading ideas in Greek philosophy, especially for the Stoics who thought of a divine reason permeating the universe, ordering all things and coming to a focus in every human mind. In Hebrew thought it is by the word that God creates the universe. In the first chapter of Genesis God says 'Let there be', and what he lets be comes into existence. It is also the divine word that comes to the prophets, giving insight into the divine purpose. It is possible that the author of the prologue was also influenced by the wisdom literature, for both wisdom and word are hypostasized, thought of in personal terms. Furthermore, both wisdom and the *logos* are pictured as being at once part of God and yet going out from God. In any case, the prologue could just as easily be applied to wisdom as it is to the word: 'In the beginning was wisdom, and wisdom was with God, and wisdom was God.'

Some Christian thinkers have seen in the description of wisdom in the Hebrew Scriptures a reference to the Holy Spirit. The third-century theologian Irenaeus, for example, distinguishes between the word, the eternal Son and wisdom, the Holy Spirit. It is through the operation of both these that God makes the world. Patrick Sherry, in *Spirit and Beauty*, sees a particular connection between the Holy Spirit and beauty. But this is a theme that need not be pursued here. According to traditional orthodoxy all that is said about one person of the Trinity can equally be said about the others. Wisdom, as well as word, is incarnate in Jesus. The Christian conviction is that this eternal word and wisdom 'has become flesh' in the person of Jesus Christ. What we see in Jesus is the wisdom by whom all things were made, that same eternal wisdom by which our lives are ordered and beautified.

This wisdom came to his own and his own received him not. We are all his own, his own people. As there is a hiddenness of the divine glory in the darkness of the world, so there is a contradiction between the wisdom of God revealed in Christ and the spurious wisdom of the world. So often we do not discern the wisdom of God and in Christ: we crucify it.

In the New Testament it is Paul who puts forward this thought most strongly. It seems clear that it was the wonderful poetry about eternal wisdom in the wisdom literature which gave him a way in to thinking about the eternity of Christ. When writing to the Corinthians Paul reminded them that, according to human standards, none of them could be regarded as powerful or aristocratic but the truth of Christ was making its way in the world through their lowliness. This was all of a piece with the way God has worked in Christ. It is through the humility of the Incarnation, the humiliation of the Crucifixion, that God is overcoming the evil in the world. Christ is 'the wisdom of God' but this wisdom stands in sharp contrast to, in contradiction of, a wordly understanding of wisdom and success. Nevertheless, the wisdom of God in Christ is the truth which will prevail. 'For the foolishness of God is wiser than men, and the weakness of God is stronger than men' (1 Corinthians 1.25).

Christ is the wisdom of God because his being is one with God, and in the Incarnation he lived out his life in an unbroken union with his heavenly Father. The glory of God in Christ was for the most part hidden. The wisdom of God in Christ contradicted the standards of the world. Yet in him is eternal wisdom, the wisdom and love that made the stars. Christ takes our lives into God and orders them in a pattern of beauty. He is seeking to win over all people, to draw them to the beauteous fount of their being, the glorious goal of their longing. He is the crucified Lord of the dance whose music can still be heard.

> They cut me down
> And I leap up high;
> I am the life
> That'll never, never die;

Eternal Wisdom

I'll live in you
If you'll live in me:
I am the Lord
Of the Dance, said he.[8]

The concept of wisdom needs to come much more to the fore in Christian thought and practice today. It was of crucial importance for the early Church and its position needs to be recovered. For wisdom holds together what we are always in danger of splitting asunder: beauty, rational order and goodness. God is beautiful, 'She is more beautiful than the sun'. This beauty is expressed in the rhythms, patterns and structures of the universe. It is also to be reflected in the right ordering of our lives. When our lives are at one with the purpose of God for us, when we hear the divine music and join in the dance, we too have an ordered beauty. In and through wisdom, God, the material world and the way we live are brought together. Aesthetics, rationality and morality are joined. Scientific exploration, artistic creation and behaviour exhibit the same characteristics of beauty, order and rationality. All can be referred to in terms of music and dancing.

All this said, there is still the most decisive fact of all, which disrupts and turns everything upside-down. For it is Christ, the lowly one, the crucified one, the fool, who reveals true wisdom; who is indeed the wisdom of God. The Christian has a distinctive perspective which leaves the believer in a state of creative tension with the accepted nostrums of the world.

It was in the 1960s, particularly with the musical *Godspell*, that the idea of Christ as a clown or fool became popular. But it does in fact have a long and sophisticated history both in theology and the arts. In modern painting the portraits of Christ by Rouault have some of the characteristics of a clown, whilst his portrait of a clown appears Christ-like. It is, however, Cecil Collins who has made the theme of the fool distinctively his own. It is a central, recurring theme in his paintings. He did not

The Crucifixion 1952 by Cecil Collins. The British Museum.
© *The Estate of Cecil Collins. Photo Clive Hicks.*

do many paintings on specifically Christian themes but he did do one pen and brown ink drawing of a crucifixion. On one side of the Cross are some stiff figures, bristling with weapons like long sharp thorns. On the other side is a line of fools, beating drums and coming to console their fellow fool on the Cross. Christ on the Cross leans towards them, seeming about to step away and join their dancing line.[9] Collins tries to bring out what the New Testament affirms, that the foolishness of God is wiser than the so-called wisdom of humanity. This foolishness invites us to follow him in the dance even when we are on our own Cross.

Francis Bacon and Olivier Messiaen both died on the same day, 28 April 1992. Bacon, for all his lovable personal qualities, including his indifference to wealth and great generosity to his friends, painted with a sense of 'exhilarated despair'. Messiaen, the most influential composer of his time, was sustained above all by 'the verities of our catholic faith'. Although he had a traumatic time as a prisoner of war, he had a very simple ambition in life: to spread joy through his music and to contradict the misery of this century. As a friend, the composer George Benjamin, put it: 'His reaction to the evil he encountered in the Second World War was to show examples of light, colour and joy.' Most of his major works have explicitly religious titles, such as 'The Heavenly Banquet', 'The Ascension', 'Birth of the Lord' and so on.

Every art form has its own proper integrity and cannot easily be translated into another. Moreover, the effort to spell out the meaning of a particular work is always difficult and nearly always unsatisfactory. Mahler drew up a programme for his second symphony 'The Resurrection' in 1896. He was very doubtful about this exercise and wrote:

We find ourselves faced with the important question of *how* and indeed *why* music should be interpreted in words at all ... as long as my experience can be summed up in words, I

77

write no music about it; my need to express myself musically — symphonically — begins at the point where the dark feelings hold sway, at the door which leads into the 'other world' — the world at which things are no longer separated by space and time.

On the day of the performance Mahler's doubts grew and he reverted to his earlier revulsion for programme notes. He wrote to his wife:

I only drew up the programme as a crutch for a cripple. It can give only a superficial indication ... in fact, as religious doctrines do, it leads directly to a flattening and coarsening, and in the long run to such distortion that the work ... is utterly unrecognizable.

Mahler is being somewhat unfair to religious doctrines, which are indispensable in their proper place. They do not pretend to be art. But art too, unavoidably and quite properly, expresses a particular perspective on life and a special feeling for it. The music of Messiaen is no more propaganda for the Christian faith than Francis Bacon's paintings were for atheism. But the works of neither artist were value-free. From the perspective of this book, it is the music of Messiaen that expresses the more profound truth. Despite everything, and it is a very big everything, the music of God can be heard and one day all things will be drawn into the dance.

Notes

1 See Anthony Harvey, *Strenuous Commands* (SCM, 1990).

2 Umberto Eco, *Art and Beauty in the Middle Ages* (Yale, 1986), pp. 18–19.

3 Simone Weil, *Waiting on God* (Fontana, 1959), p. 113.

4 Simone Weil, *Gravity and Grace* (Routledge & Kegan Paul, 1963), p. 135.

5 Boethius, *The Consolation of Philosophy*, VIII (Loeb Classical Library, 1973), p. 227.

6 Ray Monk, *Ludwig Wittgenstein* (Vintage, 1991), p. 44.

7 T. S. Eliot, 'East Coker' (line 128) in *Four Quartets* (Faber, 1959).

8 From Sydney Carter's hymn 'Lord of the Dance'.

9 William Anderson, *Cecil Collins* (Barrie & Jenkins, 1990), p. 81.

S I X

౸౸౸౸౸౸౸౸౸౸౸

Uncreated Light

L ight is a universal symbol. The contrast between light
and darkness plays a role in all religions. In some the sun
is a central reality. For example, in Egypt, Rā the Sun God
was worshipped as the giver of life in this world and the bringer
of life in the next. In Plato's *Republic* the sun is a symbol for the
source of all intellectual, moral and spiritual illumination.

The image of light is no less important, perhaps more so, in
Christianity. This importance, at least in the Orthodox Churches, is due in significant measure to St Gregory Palamas
(1296–1359) who was a monk, Archbishop and theologian,
living at various times in Constantinople, Thessalonica and
Mount Athos. Gregory Palamas drew a distinction between
God's essence, which is unknowable and unshareable, and the
divine energies through which God does make himself known
to us and through which he changes our nature. The most
important of these divine energies is God's uncreated light. This
uncreated light was above all seen irradiating Christ at the
Transfiguration.

We are most of all conscious of physical light without which
there could be no life. So it is natural to think of light as a

symbol of God, especially in bringing us spiritual insight. But Gregory Palamas was not happy to think of uncreated light simply as a symbol, a way of talking. God really *is* uncreated light as he manifests himself to us. This is what Peter, John and James saw in Christ on Mount Tabor. This is what the mystics sometimes experience. Perhaps then we should say that the uncreated light of God is the reality and daylight a sign or sacrament of this.

This uncreated light is above all things beautiful. Gregory writes of the archetype, the one in whose image we are made, in these words: 'The superluminous splendour of the beauty of the archetype — the very formless form of the divine loveliness, which deifies man.'[1]

In the Western Church in mediaeval times light was also a valued concept, integrally related to divine beauty. Mediaeval people loved light, as we know from their brightly coloured costumes, the glorious stained glass windows of the churches and the lovely illuminated manuscripts, with their bold and sharply contrasting colours. Not surprisingly they sought the source of this light and its beauty in God himself. Mention was made earlier of the question which has troubled people from Plato onwards, namely how beauty can be both proportion and light. If both are the lineaments of beauty, how are they related? Grosseteste, who led the way for all scholastic philosophers from St Bonaventure to St Thomas Aquinas, defined light as the greatest and best of all proportions.

Today, as we picture light in terms of a combination of waves and particles, this view has even more plausibility. For both waves and particles assume intervals, regular intervals, and this is an expression of form or pattern.

However understood, light is an essential element in beauty. In nature we rejoice in the light on the underside of leaves or on water, light in the sky or highlighting certain colours. The play of light and shadow, chiaroscuro, has long been part of the artist's repertoire and with the French Impressionists light became central to artistic expression. The Impressionists, painting outdoors, tried to capture the fugitive effects of light on landscape, water and buildings. The attractiveness of Impressionist painting has particularly to do with light and colour. Although the Impressionists had no influence on Van Gogh he had an approach to colour that was explicitly religious. He wrote to his brother Theo to say:

> I want to paint men and women with that something of the eternal which the halo used to symbolize, and which we seek to confer by the actual radiance and vibration of our colourizing.[2]

So we rejoice in the beauty of God's uncreated light, creating the light by which we see both physically and spiritually. 'In thy light shall we see light' (Psalm 36.9).

The Christian conviction is that this light has flooded through to us in Christ. He is 'light of light' as the Nicene Creed puts it. Not surprisingly this is a central symbol in St John's Gospel. The prologue states that in the *logos* there is life and this life is 'the light of men. The light shines in the darkness, and the darkness has not overcome it.' John came 'to bear witness to the light ... He was not the light, but came to bear witness to the light. The true light that enlightens every man was coming into the world.' In the body of the Gospel Jesus proclaims 'I am the light of the world', and the theme of light piercing our darkness, revealing everything as it really is, opening the eyes of the blind so that they can see, judging by its very presence those who do not want to see — all this is worked out in profound and subtle ways.

For Paul, too, light is central in his understanding. This light is first of all that which comes into existence by the word of God, who said 'Let there be light' and there was light. This same God shines in our hearts to give true knowledge. This is knowledge of the divine glory incarnate in Christ.

For it is the God who said, 'Let light shine out of darkness,' who has shone in our hearts to give the light of the knowledge of the glory of God in the face of Christ.

(2 Corinthians 4.6)

In the Synoptic Gospels this is set forth in the account of Christ's Transfiguration.

And after six days Jesus took with him Peter and James and John his brother, and led them up a high mountain apart. And he was transfigured before them, and his face shone like the sun, and his garments became white as light. And behold, there appeared to them Moses and Elijah, talking with him. And Peter said to Jesus 'Lord, it is well that we are here; if you wish, I will make three booths here, one for you and one for Moses and one for Elijah.' He was still speaking, when lo, a bright cloud overshadowed them, and a voice from the cloud said, 'This is my beloved Son, with whom I am well pleased; listen to him.' When the disciples heard this, they fell on their faces, and were filled with awe.   (Matthew 17.1-6)

The Transfiguration is a major feast in the Orthodox Churches but has been strangely neglected in the West. In the East this theme quickly took its place as one of the main twelve icons, setting forth the truth of God in Christ. The authoritative texts for icon painters instruct them to paint the Transfiguration first of all, bringing home to them the truth that it is only as our eyes are opened and we see Christ transfigured that we are able to be true to reality. In icons there is no natural light but a spiritual light illuminating the whole.

Christ is transfigured before the disciples. They see in him God's uncreated light. In some icons the *Mandorla* of light enclosing Christ's entire figure consists of three concentric circles, indicating the light of the whole Trinity. Gregory Palamas, arguing that the light of Tabor is indeed the true light

84

of divinity, quotes the words which are sung at the Feast of the Transfiguration: 'In your light which appeared today on Tabor, we have seen the Father as light and also the Spirit as light.'

Peter, John and James were literally bowled over in awe at the beauty they beheld. But they were able to see this beauty because their eyes were opened. Gregory Palamas quotes John of Damascus:

> Christ is transfigured, not by putting on some quality he did not possess previously, nor by changing into something he never was before, but by revealing to his disciples what he truly was, in opening their eyes and in giving sight to those who were blind. For while remaining identical to what he had been before, he appeared to the disciples in his splendour; he is indeed the true light, the radiance of glory.[3]

When Jesus was crucified, 'there was darkness over the whole land' for three hours. Christ goes into the dark. We are all in the dark, for we do not see things as they truly are. We are blind. Christ goes into the darkness that we might see. His darkness is therefore a dazzling darkness, a darkness entered for our salvation, to bring us out of that darkness. We have been called 'out of darkness into his marvellous light' (1 Peter 2.9). Often we still feel we are groping in the darkness, the darkness of our human condition or the darkness of our own wilful blindness. But now with the Psalmist we can say 'The darkness is no darkness with Thee, but the night is as clear as the day; the darkness and light to Thee are both alike' (Psalm 139.12).

The uncreated light of God irradiating in Christ on Mount Tabor is an anticipation of his Resurrection and coming again, when the whole universe will be transfigured and translucent to his glory. The city of God

> Has no need of sun or moon to shine upon it, for the glory of God is its light, and its lamp is the Lamb. By its light shall the

nations walk; and the kings of the earth shall bring their glory into it. And its gate shall never be shut by day — and there shall be no night there; they shall bring into it the glory and the honour of the nations.   (Revelation 21.23-26)

This is a theme which has engaged Christian writers in every age. Bonaventure, for example, dwells on the beauty of our resurrected selves:

> Light will shine with its four fundamental characteristics: clarity which illuminates, impassability so that it cannot corrupt, agility so that it can travel instantaneously, and penetrability so that it can pass through transparent bodies. Transfigured in heaven, the original proportions dissolved into a pure effulgence, the ideal of the *homo quadratus* returns as an aesthetic ideal in the mysticism of light.[4]

The uncreated light in Christ is bringing illumination into the darkest dungeon of our minds. The darkness is clearing away.

> Rank on rank the host of heaven
> Spreads its vanguard on the way,
> As the light of light descendeth
> From the realms of endless day,
> That the powers of hell may vanish
> As the darkness clears away.[5]

Some people seem to have a glimpse of this total illumination in their childhood. Traherne, for example, had an overwhelming sense of the glory of the primal, paradisal world. Wordsworth, too, had glimpses of this in his childhood. But strictly speaking it belongs not to childhood but to the unchanging reality of God behind, beyond and within all things and to the consummation of his kingdom in Christ. But for the most part now 'Our estranged faces miss the many splendoured thing', as the poet

The Cross in the Mountains by Caspar David Friedrich. Staatliche
Kunstsammlungen, Dresden. Photo Bridgeman Art Library.

Crucifixion No. 5 1991 by Mark Reichert. Photo Miki Slingsby.

Francis Thompson put it. Another poet, Kathleen Raine, has
written:

> Today the curtain is down,
> The veil drawn over the face,
> World only its aspect,
> Tree, brick wall, dusty leaves
>
> Of ivy, a bird
> Shaken loose from the dust
> It is the colour of. Nothing
> Means or is.
>
> Yet I saw once
> The woven light of which all these are made
> Otherwise than this. To have seen
> Is to know always.[6]

For most of us, most of the time, the curtain is down. Life
seems somewhat drab and ordinary. But occasionally, perhaps
just once, we see 'the woven light' of which all things are
made.

One of the strengths of the Christian faith is the way it can
hold together in one vision the physical and the spiritual. The
world has been created good/beautiful by God. Christ has
claimed it as his own and will raise it to eternal light and life.
This means that the material and the immaterial, the visible and
the invisible, the physical and the spiritual interpenetrate one
another. The physical world becomes radiant with eternity and
eternity is seen in terms of a transfigured physical world. This
means that all everyday experiences have a sacramental
character. One of the most beautiful ways in which the Church
has expressed this is in the evening hymns from before the
fourth century and through the ages. As night descends and we
lose the physical light the Christian heart is lifted into the

eternal light of Christ. T. S. Eliot is another who has celebrated the interconnectedness of physical and spiritual light.

O Light Invisible, we praise Thee!
Too bright for mortal vision.
O Greater Light, we praise Thee for the less; the eastern light
    our spires touch at morning,
The light that slants upon our western doors at evening,
The twilight over stagnant pools at bat-flight,
Moonlight and starlight, owl and mothlight,
Glow-worm glowlight on a grass-blade.
O Light Invisible, we worship Thee![7]

Light is a symbol with universal appeal and has a place in all religions. It is certainly central to Christian truth. St John's Gospel in particular makes Christ, the Light of the World, a leading theme. Even more important, for Christian understanding, is the Transfiguration of Christ. Peter, James and John saw Christ radiant with glory and this vision is to be understood as a revelation both of Christ's true, eternal being and of our destiny, as those whose humanity is being transfigured by our life in Christ. This is a theme which will be taken up in the last chapter. In the blackness of this world the light of Christ is for the most part hidden. But those who allow Christ to share their darkness find in him a light that guides them on their way.

God is uncreated light and our crying need is to see this. St Augustine has a famous prayer:

O Thou who art the light of the minds that know Thee,
The life of the souls that love Thee,
And the strength of the wills that serve Thee.
Help us so to know Thee that we may truly love Thee,
So to love Thee that we may fully serve Thee,
Whose service is perfect freedom.[8]

The starting point is the illumination of our minds and the cleansing of our hearts by the light of God in Christ, in order that we may truly see. Radiance is a fundamental constituent of beauty, so what we see is nothing less than the eternal beauty which in illuminating our minds draws us to himself.

Material light which gives us so much, without which there can be no life or growth or beauty, is to be seen as a sacrament of the eternal, uncreated light. In and through the light by which we physically see there is the uncreated light. Artists, in their different ways, discern and struggle to express this. For light and colour, particularly in modern painting, are so often the key components. To love the light which is in God in no way detracts from this. Rather, our appreciation is enhanced. As John Keble put it in one of his lines: 'There is no light but Thee, with Thee all beauty glows.'

Notes

1 Gregory Palamas, *The Triads* (SPCK, 1983), p. 106.

2 *The Letters of Vincent Van Gogh*, ed. Mark Roskill (Fontana, 1983), p. 286.

3 *The Triads*, p. 76.

4 St Bonaventure quoted by Umberto Eco, *Art and Beauty in the Middle Ages* (Yale, 1986), pp. 50-1.

5 Hymn 'Let all mortal flesh keep silence', from the Liturgy of St James, trans. Gerard Moultrie.

6 Kathleen Raine, poem published in *The Tablet*.

7 T. S. Eliot, 'Choruses from "The Rock", 1934' in *Complete Poems and Plays* (Faber, 1969), p. 166.

8 Based on St Augustine, *Letter* 155, 6.

S E V E N

∽∽∽∽∽∽∽∽∽∽∽∽

The Human Longing

There is a tantalizing quality about our most precious experiences. In Samuel Beckett's play *Krapp's Last Tape*, Krapp is on stage throughout, listening to tape recordings he has made of his life at the same point every year. At the heart of this yearly remembrance is the memory of a love not followed up. He was with a girl in a boat: 'We lay there without moving. But under us all moved, and moved us, gently, up and down, and from side to side.'[1] The gentle, lyrical beauty of this memory is in sharp contrast to Krapp's characteristic frustration but it only serves to increase his fury.

Krapp's rage erupts from the sense of a love/beauty that has not been followed up, that now belongs irrevocably to the past. Yet even at the time it had a tantalizing quality about it. For beauty delights us, takes us out of ourselves in appreciation and wonder, and at the same time leaves us outside. It makes us at once utterly satisfied and strangely unsatisfied.

It is this sense that runs through much of the poetry of Edward Thomas. His poem 'The Glory' begins:

> The glory of the beauty of the morning —
> The cuckoo crying over the untouched dew;

The blackbird has found it, and the dove
That tempts me on to something sweeter than love;
[...]
The glory invites me, yet it leaves me scorning
All I can ever do, all I can be,
Beside the lovely motion, shape, and hue,
The happiness I fancy fit to dwell
In beauty's presence.[2]

The poem goes on to accentuate this sense of frustration, 'Must I be content with discontent?', and ends with the words 'I cannot bite the day to the core'.

This experience is widespread, perhaps universal and can be triggered by the most familiar features of everyday life. As the Irish man of letters J. W. N. Sullivan describes it:

At such moments one suddenly sees everything with new eyes; one feels on the brink of some great revelation. It is as if we caught a glimpse of some incredibly beautiful world that lies silently about us all the time. I remember vividly my first experience of the kind when, as a boy, I came suddenly upon the quiet miracle of an ivy-clad wall glistening under a London street-lamp. I wanted to weep and I wanted to pray; to weep for the Paradise from which I had been exiled, and to pray that I might yet be made worthy of it.[3]

This sense of longing for a paradise from which we feel exiled was given uninhibited expression in the poetry, music, painting and sculpture of the Romantic Movement. Like all artistic categories the Romantic Movement has blurred edges, but artists of this period shared a reaction against what they thought of as the shallow rationalism of the Enlightenment. They wanted to go, as they felt, deeper. Eighteenth-century painters had sought the sublime in nature but to the Romantics their picturesque scenes had no hint of 'inner goings on', as

Coleridge put it. Romantic artists looked for 'something far more deeply interfused'. The universal is the deep in Romantic belief: pierce right down at one particular point and you get to the all, and the one and the all are connected. It is from this that we arrive at the alternating particularity and generality of Wordsworth's *The Prelude*. The result is that Romantic land-scapes often have a strongly religious quality to them. They transferred to landscapes something of the Protestant attitude to God. Sometimes these landscapes are manifestly symbolic, as they were with Caspar David Friedrich. His *Cross in the Mountains* still expresses a strongly religious quality, the firs and the cross silhouetted against the sky evoking a sense of the lonely soul reaching out to the Infinite. The rays of light shining out behind the mountain and the colour of the sky indicate new hope, a fresh start, resurrection. All his landscapes have an ambivalent, hallucinatory quality. Though they are full of symbols, their power is not simply in the symbols but in the 'strong intense polarity of closeness and distance, precise detail and sublime aura'.[4]

Baudelaire said that in the paintings of Delacroix he could see an 'aspiration towards the infinite'. Not surprisingly the Romantic Movement has been termed 'spilt religion'.[5] The works of the Romantic Movement reveal a sense of the solitariness of the artist and the isolation of the viewer or listener as similar feelings are evoked by the work of art. It is an isolation related to the sundering of the old bonds of commu-nity by a rapidly industrializing society. The artist's life, his subjectivity, his feelings, all come strongly to the fore. The religious certainties of the past, an integral part of the community to which artists belonged, are no more. The artist is on his own with his yearning.

For Plato the longings aroused by experiences of earthly beauty were evoked by beauty itself. We can and should move up the ladder of beauty from the physical to the spiritual to the source of all beauty, in which all beauty participates. Plotinus emphasized this point even more strongly, setting Plato's philosophy within a more consciously religious perspective. Pseudo-Dionysius, the sixth-century mystical writer who influenced late Christian thought almost as much as Plotinus, claimed (following a suggestion of Plato) that the word *kalon* (the beautiful, the fine, the good) was linked with the word *kalein* (to call), for 'beauty bids all things to itself'.

All this was meat and drink to Christians. For them, it sooner or later became obvious that God himself is the ultimate goal of the longing evoked by experiences of beauty. St Augustine is the most famous example of this, for it is the central theme of his *Confessions*. But the idea was expressed no less strongly by other writers. Gregory of Nyssa wrote of Moses:

> He shone with glory. And although lifted up through such lofty experiences, he is still unsatisfied in his desire for more. He still thirsts for that with which he constantly filled himself to capacity, and he asks to attain as if he had never partaken, beseeching God to appear to him, not according to his capacity to partake, but according to God's true being. Such an experience seems to me to belong to the soul which loves what is beautiful.
>
> Hope always draws the soul from the beauty which is seen to what is beyond, always kindles the desire for the hidden through what is constantly perceived. Therefore the ardent lover of beauty, although receiving what is always visible has an image of what he desires, yet longs to be filled with the very stamp of the archetype. And the bold request which goes up the mountains of desire asks this: to enjoy the beauty not in mirrors and reflections, but face to face.[6]

The yearning aroused by experiences of beauty is a longing for God himself, for communion with his beauty. The goal of the Christian life has sometimes been conceived as 'the beatific vision'. This conveys the idea of that which is unutterably beautiful transfixing us in rapture. Occasionally when listening to music or looking at a scene in nature or a work of art we are taken out of ourselves. 'You are the music while the music lasts.'[7] We seem to experience a timeless moment. Such moments are a pointer to the meaning of the beatific vision.

This desire for communion with the inexpressibly lovely is however only part of the reason for the intensity of longing aroused by experiences of beauty. The other part is the deep desire that we ourselves might be so changed that this beauty becomes part of us, that we become what we behold. Edward Thomas ended his poem on a note of frustration: 'I cannot bite the day to the core.' This image of looking and eating was used by Simone Weil when reflecting on the nature of beauty.

A beautiful thing involves no good except itself, in its totality as it appears to us. We are drawn towards it without knowing what to ask of it. It offers us its own existence. We do not desire anything else, we possess it, and yet we still desire something. We do not in the least know what it is. We want to get behind beauty, but it is only a surface. It is like a mirror that sends us back our own desire for goodness. It is a sphinx, an enigma, a mystery which is painfully tantalizing. We should like to feed upon it but it is merely something to look at, it appears only from a certain distance. The great trouble in human life is that looking and eating are two different operations. Only beyond the sky, in the country inhabited by God, are they one and the same operation.[8]

In human life we look and find some satisfaction in the contemplation, but we ask for more. Beauty is a mirror that sends back our own desire for greater goodness. We look but we also want to eat. We want that at which we are looking to become part of us, we want to be changed into that which we are contemplating. Here looking and eating are separate. But in the consummation of all things they will be one and the same operation. C. S. Lewis wrote:

We do not want merely to *see* beauty ... We want something else that can hardly be put into words — to be united with the beauty we see, to pass into it, to receive it into ourselves, to bathe in it, to become part of it. That is why we have peopled air and earth and water with gods and goddesses and nymphs and elves — that, though we cannot, yet these projections can, enjoy themselves that beauty, grace and power of which nature is the image ... For if we take the imagery of Scripture seriously, if we believe that God will one day *give* us the morning star and calls us to *put on* the splendour of the sun, then we may surmise that both the ancient myth and the modern poetry, so false as history, may be very near the truth as prophecy. At present we are on the outside of the world, the wrong side of the door. We discern the freshness and purity of morning, but they do not make us fresh and pure. We cannot mingle with the splendours we see. But all the leaves of the New Testament are rustling with the rumour that it will not always be so. Some day, God willing, we shall get *in*. When human souls have become perfect in voluntary obedience as the inanimate creation is in its lifeless obedience, then they will put on its glory, or rather that greater glory which nature is only the first sketch ... We are summoned to pass in through nature, beyond her, into that splendour which she fitfully reflects.[9]

This striking passage from C. S. Lewis seems somewhat lonely in Western thought. But his theme has always been fundamental to Orthodox theology and spirituality. The doctrine or rather the vision of theiosis, divinization, is central. This understanding of human beings says that through the grace of God in Christ we are to be totally changed, to become like him. We are to take on his beauty. We are to become light as he is light. It is this that icons of the saints in Orthodox iconography try to convey. For icons do not depict the saints in their earthly but in their heavenly reality. Their human reality is transfigured. If this all sounds too heady, a long way from received Protestantism, it is firmly there in Paul. He wrote:

> And we all, with unveiled face, beholding the glory of the Lord, are being changed into his likeness from one degree of glory to another.   (2 Corinthians 3.18)

The longing evoked by experiences of beauty is a deep desire for God himself. It is a longing that we ourselves might become all beauty, all light, all glory, in and through the glory of God shining in the face of Jesus Christ. This is our vision and our hope. As it is put in the *Homilies of St Macarius*:

> Just as the Lord's body was glorified, when he went up the mountain and was transfigured into the glory of God and into infinite light, so the saints' bodies are also glorified and shine as lightning ... 'The glory which thou has given me I have given to them.' (John 17.22): just as many lamps are lit from one flame, so the bodies of the saints, being members of Christ, must needs be what Christ is, and nothing else. Our human nature is transformed into the power of God, and it is kindled into fire and light.[10]

So, as the Psalmist puts it:

> But as for me, I will behold thy presence in righteousness; and when I awake up after thy likeness, I shall be satisfied with it.   (Psalm 17.15)

As human beings we are beset by strange longings for we know not quite what. Poets witness to this. But so do countless ordinary people who would not necessarily consider themselves religious, for they have given accounts of their deepest experiences to researchers.[11] Not surprisingly, Christians claim that we have this yearning because God exists as the ground of our being and the goal of our longing. He is our true good in whom we find our full happiness and lasting fulfilment. Sometimes this longing can be displaced, as in the Romantic Movement, when nature rather than God became the prime focus for many.

Our human longing is first of all to be united with God, to be in deeper communion with him. Secondly, it is to be changed into his likeness. We want to become what we long for. Edward Thomas and Simone Weil express this idea in the strong imagery of eating beauty. C. S. Lewis writes of being clothed by beauty. Although this can seem somewhat exotic to people brought up in a Western Christian tradition it has always been fundamental to the Orthodox Churches, with their notion of divinization or theiosis. As Gregory Palamas put it: 'We are to be made beautiful by the creative and primordial beauty, and illumined by the radiance of God.'[12]

It is in this light that we should understand the Eucharist or Holy Communion. Understandably, many people today are put off this service because of its cannibalistic imagery. We cannot escape the startling nature of phrases like eating the body of Christ or drinking his blood. But if we begin in heaven rather than earth it all looks rather different. God has created us, has given us a life of our own. But he also wills, in response to our desire, to fill us with his own life. Indeed what other life is there to fill us with? Moment by moment our being flows from him. Moment by moment grace in so many ways comes our way. The divine beauty wishes to fill us with himself and irradiate us with his own beauty. 'You are what you eat' has become a slogan but it points to a truth Christians would not deny. We are invited to take the divine beauty into our very being. Human meals, however sociable, are but a faint reflection of that fundamental truth. Even human meals are, of course, much more than a means of taking in calories. We take in the atmosphere at table, the conviviality and friendship and love. This has effects, for good and ill, upon young children. But at the table of God we take in God himself. We are in a holy communion with him and one another. God feeds us with himself — the bread of life, the food of immortality — and we are changed into his likeness from one degree of glory to another. This is the heavenly/earthly reality. Of this the Eucharist is symbol and sacrament.

Notes

1 Samuel Beckett, *Krapp's Last Tape* (Faber, 1959), p. 17.

2 Edward Thomas, 'The Glory' in *Collected Poems* (Faber, 1974), p. 64.

3 J. W. N. Sullivan, *But for the Grace of God*, quoted in *The New Year of Grace*, ed. Victor Gollancz (Gollancz, 1961), p. 379.

4 Hugh Honour, *Romanticism* (Penguin, 1991), pp. 77-8.

5 See especially chapter 8 of *Romanticism*.

6 *Gregory of Nyssa: The Life of Moses* (Paulist, New York, 1978), p. 114.

7 T. S. Eliot, 'The Dry Salvages', *Four Quartets* (Faber, 1954), p. 46.

8 Simone Weil, *Waiting on God* (Fontana, 1959), p. 121.

9 C. S. Lewis, 'The Weight of Glory' in *Transposition and Other Addresses* (Bles, 1949), p. 31.

10 *Homilies of St Macarius* quoted by Kallistos Ware, *The Orthodox Way* (Mowbray, 1979), p. 171.

11 The research carried out by the Sir Alistair Hardy Centre at Oxford shows that a very high percentage of people claim to have had an experience of the mystical, the sublime, the ineffable.

12 Gregory Palamas, *The Triads* (SPCK, 1983), p. 33.

EIGHT

∽∽∽∽∽∽∽∽∽∽∽∽

The Spiritual in Art

All works of art, whatever their content, have a spiritual dimension. They can be a source of strength and consolation at times of difficulty. An ordinand I knew lost his faith in a way that left him desolate. He got through many difficult months by a sustained reading of Shakespeare. This was not just as a distraction from his pain; rather, what he read in Shakespeare reflected and gave depth to his own feelings about life at that time: its anguish and tragedy, delight and humour, its pointlessness and grandeur.

Millions find delight and inspiration listening to classical music. Millions more find that it is through literature, theatre, opera, film and the visual arts that they derive insight and meaning as well as pleasure. For many people the arts are the most important feature of their lives, giving force to Tillich's view that we all have an 'ultimate concern', that which we take with utter seriousness. In contrast, for a variety of reasons, what is offered by the churches can seem stale and thin. John Osborne said once that he would rather go to a church service than to a performance in the West End. Heartening though this view is for a church person, it is not one which is widely shared. For too many it is the arts, rather than institutional religion, which engage them most seriously.

The spiritual dimension to great art, whatever its subject matter, is related to a number of factors. First, all art depends on form and artistic form is a human reflection of the work of the divine *logos*. I argued in Chapter 2 that proportion and balance, harmony and wholeness are characteristic features of the beautiful. In Chapter 5 I wrote about the work of eternal wisdom. The divine *logos*, eternal wisdom, shapes every element in creation. So, at every level, we find symmetry and pattern. St Augustine, preaching on the prologue of St John's Gospel, said of the eternal wisdom:

> For no form, no structure, no agreement of parts, no substance whatever that can have weight, number, measure, exists but by that word, and by that creator word, to whom it is said, 'Thou hast ordered all things in measure and in number and in weight.'[1]

Augustine there quotes Wisdom 11.20, a text that meant much not only to him but to the mediaeval Church in its analysis of beauty.

Human beings, made in the image of God, share in the divine creativity. We also have the capacity for creative, beautiful ordering. In particular, artists of every kind share in the work of the divine artist by giving form to recalcitrant matter. They make music of inchoate sounds and speech of incoherent babble. They give shape to the shapeless and in so doing reflect the work of eternal wisdom.

To say that all art has form is not to say that those forms are unchangeable. On the contrary, artists in every age experiment with new forms. But new forms are still forms. Abstract art is just as much (in fact rather more) an art of pure form than the art of the Impressionists. The musical revolutions that took place in Europe before the 1914–18 War struck most listeners at the time as strange, even alien. Now we take such music for granted and discern form in what once was heard as cacophony. Theatre may become more experimental and move away from the three unities of time, space and character that were regarded as essential by Aristotle, but it will still have form.

Kandinsky in his book *Concerning the Spiritual in Art*, first published in 1914 and something of a manifesto for abstract art, related the spiritual dimension closely to form.[2] In particular, along with many others, he believed that all art aspired to the condition of music. For him this music was an expression of an inner music, the music of the soul and the universe. Where Kandinsky fails to convince is in his attempt to relate colour and music to the inner dimension in a way that is precise and almost mathematical.

Nevertheless, the form itself has spiritual significance. The artist Clive Bell argued that in seeing the significant form of things the artist somehow glimpses 'ultimate reality'. Even Paul Evdokimov in his diatribe against modern art as a sign of the disintegration and degradation of our society could say:

> Abstract art is an answer to the sought-after purity of the soul, the nostalgia of lost innocence, the desire to find at least a ray or a burst of colour which has not been soiled by an earthly face.[3]

There is no art without form. Equally, in all but the most abstract work (and perhaps even here) there is content. Some aspect of the created order is caught and held in the sunlight of human awareness. Some words used about James Joyce have often been used about Samuel Beckett: 'Here form *is* content, content *is* form.' Beckett's plays are indeed characterized by brilliant form, essentially of a very simple kind, namely many different kinds of repetition. But it is quite absurd to suggest that there is no content. A particular feeling for and view of life is powerfully and movingly conveyed.

The theme of Chapter 6 was that the luminous element in beauty has its source in the uncreated light of God himself. In the visual arts this luminosity takes shape as the play of light and shade, and in the rich variety of colours. The primary expression of uncreated light, however, is in the intellectual and spiritual illumination it brings. This is first of all knowledge of God himself. But it is the same uncreated light who enables us to see life as it is and as it ought to be. This light is fundamental to art, for genuine art shifts our perceptions and shapes the way we see the world.

Those who like paintings find that certain landscapes are seen through eyes trained by paintings of them. It is not simply that a landscape looks like a Corot or Constable or Cézanne, as though we see the landscape and it then brings to mind a painting we have seen of a similar scene. Rather, having studied a painting, having our sensibility shaped by it, we cannot help seeing particular landscapes in terms of those paintings. A similar effect is produced by all art. Horses grazing in a meadow can seem like the retired race horses of Philip Larkin's poem 'At Grass', or Edwin Muir's 'Horses' about horses that survive a nuclear holocaust. Certain people will 'be' Winnie of Beckett's *Happy Days* or some other character from a play or novel that has affected them. All art gives expression to a feeling for life and this inevitably communicates itself. After we have read some novels or seen certain plays well performed life is literally never the same again.

The whole person is involved in this shift of perception. I argued in Chapter 4 that, except in the case of purely decorative art, we cannot separate considerations of beauty from either truth or goodness. It is as rational, moral beings that a work of art impels us to 'see things'. In his autobiography Arthur Miller describes the effect that his play *Death of a Salesman* had on people:

As sometimes happened later on during the run, there was no applause at the final curtain at the first performance. Strange things began to go on in the audience. With the curtain down, some people stood to put their coats on then sat down again, some, especially men, were bent forward covering their faces, and others were openly weeping. People crossed the theatre to stand quietly talking with one another. I was standing at the back and saw a distinguished looking elderly man being led up the aisle: he was talking excitedly into the ear of what seemed to be his male secretary or assistant. This, I learnt, was Bernard Gimbel, head of the department store chain, who that night gave an order that no one in his store was to be fired for being over-age.[4]

Plays may not have that effect too often. But I have been to half a dozen performances which have deeply affected the way I see life. The same is true for a certain number of novels and poems. In principle, every work of art has this potential.

Art first of all makes us see the 'isness' of what is before us, whether we like what we see or not. Gerard Manley Hopkins, drawing on Duns Scotus, was acutely conscious of *haecceitas*. This is not just the 'thisness' of things, of which the mystics have been so aware: the fact that things exist at all, springing up moment by moment from the source of all being. *haecceitas* is the particular, unique way in which everything exists. A still-life painting can sometimes convey this sense and so can a poem, a novel or a play simply by depicting what is there, truthfully, without adornment or comment. Sister Wendy Beckett, a perceptive Christian writer on art, has written that though there are few religious elements in the art of most of our contemporaries their art is often beautifully and deeply spiritual. Referring to some contemporary painters she writes:

Sally Warner, an American, draws trees, brushwood, stone, and they are luminous with God. William Bailey, another, older American, paints jugs and kitchen vessels and a wooden table with a sacramental strength that is overpowering. Avigdor Arikha, an Israeli, can show us a bare wall, a broom, bottles, young women, rooms and stairways or scattered shoes and socks, and the viewer is seized with the wonder of what is seen. Arikha makes no attempt to glorify his shoes and socks. They lie crumpled and shabby, not even, we feel, arranged for our viewing. But the artist has seen their simple quiddity, their truth to their own nature, their materiality, as purely beautiful. His charcoal hovers around their forms with both love and reverence.[5]

The capacity to see what is there, without illusion, self-indulgence, fantasy or denigration is integrally related to the capacity to love. As David Hockney has said, 'All art, all creativity, comes from love'.

The capacity to attend to what is before us, to attend to the quiddity — the very essence of a thing as it makes itself visible to us — is basic to the artistic enterprise. Indeed, our human capacity to see things, or to describe, draw or paint them, is an essential aspect of their existence. Oliver Soskice, a painter and writer on art, has explored what it is for a painter to spend hours and days before a bottle or an apple. He writes:

Painting does not record: instead it finds in the activity of colour the act by which things are made visible. Take an imaginary still-life: there are the basic elements — apples on a plate, the canvas and the colours ... What you want is to persuade the apples to identify their central activity — to exist — with what should be the activity of colours, bringing each other into being as a luminous surface. A benign strife must run between what is purely but emptily visible — i.e. colour and *things*, which have to be coaxed to the point where they become their own truest unfolding as the open instantaneity of a coloured surface plane.

Quoting Rilke and Hölderlin, he believes that they

Corroborate the notion that the existence of the world cannot be separated from its luminosity, so this luminosity imposes itself on human beings as the vehicle through which it can occur, and that this imposition is what makes us human.

And this activity, this attention to the quiddity of what is before us, coaxing it into visibility brings us up against the mystery of existence itself.

Inexpressibly other from the nature of every being, existence is received as the unreachable beckoning horizon within stones, the sky, brickwork rained upon, daylight, pools of reflecting water, apples in a bowl. A painter may spend a lifetime trying to translate this strange, innermost utterance of visible things. Yet inexpressibly other is not the same as inexpressibly alien, because the unknown pole of everything is precisely what imposes our humanity upon us.[6]

So, if the spiritual dimension in art is related first of all to its form, it is secondly due to art's capacity to put before us what simply is, in all its uniqueness. It is in the unique, the irreducible that there shines forth for Hopkins the glory of God, and for others the same can be said. The third aspect of the spiritual dimension of art is an extension of this awareness. It is to see what is depicted in its wider meaning and significance.

Plato believed that all art was a form of imitation (*mimesis*) but imitation at a third remove from the archetype. The archetype of say a bed, its ideal form, exists (according to Plato) as a metaphysical reality. A physical bed imitates this insofar as it partakes of the ideal form. At a third remove is the bed in a painting, copying the physical bed but inadequately, so Plato thought. The person who designs and constructs the physical bed has a far better understanding of what it should be than the painter.

Plotinus rightly indicated a higher view of art by pointing out that an artist need not simply imitate the physical bed at third remove from the ideal but can, through mind and spirit, go as it were direct to the ideal and seek to convey this in art. In short, there is a mental, imaginative, creative element at work. This, far from making art inferior to the physical, elevates it to a metaphysical and indeed religious plane. At various stages in history this understanding of art has been to the fore. Michelangelo, for example, believed that all earthly beauty takes its attributes 'from the sacred fount whence all men come'. He wrote of his work:

No block of marble but it does not hide
The concept living in the artist's mind —
Pursuing it inside that form, he'll guide his hand to shape
what reason has defined.[7]

The point of this stress on the idea is not to suggest that it has to refer to some ideal, as its original proponents believed, but that the intellectual, imaginative, spiritual element in art is of crucial importance. Van Gogh painted his bed, a bed which had particular significance for him personally. We do not just see a copy or a photograph or a design. We see a bed shimmering with all the reality it had for Van Gogh. In short, art is somehow related to 'the meaning' and 'truth' of things, not just as they can be copied but as they can be envisaged in the mind of the creative artist. And this mind will reflect, in however cloudy a manner, the way God sees things.

The ideas of meaning and truth are highly contentious in philosophy, let alone in their application to the arts. The main objection felt by many to works of art being spelt out in terms of their meaning has less to do with philosophy than with sensibility. People who say that the meaning of a poem or novel or play is really '*this*', and who then give it a Freudian or religious or anti-religious or political meaning, too often reduce what is complex, dense, rich and many-faceted to something trite and banal. Nevertheless, every work, even those that seem value-free (for example the plays of Chekhov), are in fact suffused with and expressive of value. Inevitably, therefore, they suggest certain things, they entice us to see a person or a situation in a certain light. Furthermore, this suggestion is inevitably related to life as we know it and will therefore strike us as true or false. This does not mean that the standpoint of the author — philosophical, religious or political — has to be shared. You do not need to be a Marxist to appreciate Brecht or a Roman Catholic to like Evelyn Waugh. Nevertheless, the question about whether a work succeeds artistically cannot be totally divorced from its relationship to life.

Patrick White's novel *Riders in the Chariot* depicts the crucifixion of a Jew, Himmelfarb, in Australian suburbia. One critic, R. F. Brissendon, has written:

It is patently White's intention to suggest, through Himmel-farb's 'crucifixion', that within an ordinary suburb the same evil forces which animated Nazi Germany exist, at least potentially. The intention, unfortunately, is not completely realized. One reason may be that societies just do differ qualitatively: the hell of Auschwitz and Buchenwald is not the hell of Australian suburbia, and to equate them must inevitably seem grotesquely disproportionate. Ordinary people may behave monstrously, but only under extraordinary pressures, and these do not at present appear to operate in Australia. Such communal cruelty as does occur is usually the cruelty of neglect, ignorance or an amused and shallow contempt.

Patrick White won the Nobel Prize for Literature and *Riders in the Chariot* is one of his finest novels. It is a complex, subtle, sometimes difficult work. Nevertheless, Brissendon rightly saw in the novel an intention to suggest something. Secondly, he judges that from a literary point of view White's intention is not completely realized. This is, he thinks, because White has not understood Australia and Nazi Germany correctly. Another critic, William Walsh, has disagreed with Brissendon's view of the book. He suggests that Brissendon is taking a sociological view of White's undertaking whereas

> He is not concerned, surely, with the relative merits of two societies but with the indissoluble connection of forms of human evil. Each, whether extreme or near, comes from the corrupt will or the clouded understanding. Each in its way is a mode of non-being.[8]

Yet, we might say, if there is an indissoluble connection between different forms of human evil then it will be necessary to show that there are certainly similarities between Nazi Germany and Australian suburbia, and that there is the potential in suburban vices for the malevolent evil that poisoned the world in the Nazi period.

The point here is not to judge the success or the failure of the novel. It is simply to indicate that in making a literary judgement about the artistic success or failure of a particular work, there will be an appeal to our experience of the world. It is because all works of art relate, in one way or another, to our world that they can illuminate it and change the way we see it.

In his enigmatic remarks on aesthetics Wittgenstein drew a distinction between what can be said and what can be shown. This distinction was fundamental to his early philosophy but he related it no less passionately to his understanding of art. Art shows something. In the case of White's novel we might say that it shows a particular kind of evil at work as well as a mystic goodness. Wittgenstein wrote that works of art see objects under the aspect of eternity.

The work of art is the object seen *sub specie aeternitatis*; and the good life is the world seen *sub specie aeternitatis*.
This is the connection between art and ethics.
The usual way of looking at things sees objects as it were from the midst of them, the view *sub specie aeternitatis* from outside.
In such a way that they have the whole world as background.[9]

We cannot of course grasp 'the whole world as background', or anything near it, particularly if we are expected to take in all time and space. So the extent to which an artist can really depict something from the standpoint of eternity is extremely limited. Nevertheless, that is the thrust of what an artist does, whether aware of it or not. That which the artist struggles to express in words or stone or music reflects, in however a cloudy or distorted fashion, the larger, divine perspective, of all time and beyond time.

If all genuine art has a spiritual dimension there is also within this a distinctive tradition of ostensibly spiritual art. By this is not meant Christian art: art that uses Christian symbols or depicts Christian scenes; or religious art which might do the same for another religion. Rather, this tradition seeks to indicate through symbols the eternal reality behind, beyond and within this world. In Britain it is a tradition best represented by William Blake, both in his poetry and paintings, and in the modern world by the poet Kathleen Raine and the painter Cecil Collins. This is the tradition of mystical Platonism expressed in artistic form. Platonism has been a great ally of Christian thought and art. Nevertheless, in the mainstream it has always been anchored to the sea-bed of the incarnation of God in Jesus. This Christian Platonism has looked to Plato to open up the realm of eternity and to Jesus, as the incarnation of eternity in time. This has set up a necessary and creative tension. The mystical Platonism represented by someone like Cecil Collins, however, sits more lightly to belief in a unique incarnation in Christ whilst seeking to evoke, through a variety of symbols, the reality of the eternal world. Such art has its own particular point, purpose and appeal. There is an altar frontal by Cecil Collins in Chichester Cathedral and Canon Keith Walker commissioned a glass window by him for the church of All Saints, Basingstoke. Such art is a valuable friend of Christian faith.

Yet this chapter's theme is that all genuine art has a spiritual dimension. It is totally misleading to think that only art that tries to depict the eternal dimension through symbols has this quality. Cézanne was a regular church-goer for the last fifteen years of his life and religion was increasingly important to him as he got older. Nevertheless, he did not attempt religious themes in his painting. He concentrated instead upon landscape and still-life. Yet through his delight in the colour and shapes of the world he delights also in God.

The spiritual in art is related to three features. First, the artist, in trying to shape words or stone or music or any other material into a work of art, reflects the work of the divine *logos*, whose ordered beauty in the universe comes to a focus in each human mind. Secondly, the radiant splendour of the eternal wisdom illuminates our mind, enabling us to see all things springing up from the fount of being in their unique, glorious particularity. Those who produce works of art and those who appreciate them are illuminated by this light. Thirdly, this uncreated light not only reveals things as they are but shows them in relation to a wider meaning and truth: imperfectly grasped, only a flicker or a fragment of the truth, yet nevertheless an aspect of God's truth. This is true of even the most abstract art. Bridget Riley has said that

> If painting is to be a work, a work that aspires to the condition of art, it is obliged to express the tenor of ex- istence. There is no escaping the changing pulse of our

experience ... Art has to be expressive of the urgency and failure, love and inadequacy that drive human endeavour.[10]

Bridget Riley's own recent collection of paintings, abstract as they are, are charged with extraordinary hope and encouragement. It is not by chance, I suspect, that they bear titles like *Certain Day* and *New Day*.

This spiritual aspect of all works of art awakens something even in those like Peter Fuller, who regarded himself as an incorrigible atheist. In our time especially it has a particular spiritual appeal. It plays the role of Virgil in Dante's *Divine Comedy*, for there it is the pagan poet who comes to help Dante. Dorothy Sayers has written:

Dante is so far gone in sin and error that divine grace can no longer move him directly; but there is still something left in him which is capable of responding to the voice of poetry and of human reason; and this, under grace, may yet be used to lead him back to God.

Yet religious propagandists must always beware of using the spirituality inherent in art for their own purpose. Charles Williams, a lover of Dante and a novelist in his own right, saw this clearly. Virgil can help Dante but he cannot be commanded.

Beatrice has to ask Virgil to go; she cannot command him, though she puts her trust in his 'fair speech'. Religion itself cannot order poetry about; the grand art is wholly autonomous.[11]

This is one of the delightful ironies by which God saves us from ourselves. True art always has a spiritual dimension. Yet if religion tries to turn it into propaganda the spiritual could slip away. Works of art inescapably witness, by their truth and

113

beauty, to their fount and origin in God himself. Yet religion, always in danger of being corrupted and corrupting, does not have this art at its beck and call. It cannot use it for its own ends. It can, however, recognize and praise both the artist and the artist's God, and, where appropriate, seek to express its own deepest truths in works of truth and beauty.

The artist may or may not have a professed religious faith. From an artistic point of view that does not affect the spirituality of the work produced. What does matter is a fundamental seriousness, fierce artistic integrity, of the kind thought essential by Hopkins and Wittgenstein. It is this that enables a person to bring together beauty and truth in a way that conveys some aspect of reality.

Notes

1 St Augustine, *On the Gospel According to St John*, Tractate I in *The Nicene and Post-Nicene Fathers* (Eerdman, 1983), p. 11.

2 Wassily Kandinsky, *Concerning the Spiritual in Art* (Dover, New York, 1977).

3 Paul Evdokimov, *The Art of the Icon: A Theology of Beauty* (Oakwood, California, 1990), p. 94.

4 Arthur Miller, *Timebends* (Methuen, 1987), p. 191.

5 Sister Wendy Beckett, 'The Spirituality of Contemporary Art', *Third Way* (September 1990), p. 8.

6 Oliver Soskice, 'Painting and the Absence of Grace', *Modern Painters* 4.1 (Spring 1991).

7 Michelangelo, 'Non ha ottimo artista alcun concetto' in *Life, Letters and Poetry* (OUP, 1987), p. 153.

8 William Walsh, *Patrick White's Fiction* (Allen and Unwin, 1977), p. 60.

9 Ray Monk, *Ludwig Wittgenstein* (Vintage, 1991), p. 143.

10 'According to Sensation': Bridget Riley in conversation with Robert Kudielka (Sidney Janis exhibition catalogue, New York, 1990).

11 Charles Williams, *The Figure of Beatrice* (Faber, 1943), p. 112.

N I N E

~~~~~~~~~~~~~

The Invisible Made Visible

Those who go to the theatre know that occasionally, perhaps only a few times in a lifetime, the performance is magical. They are totally taken out of themselves into the drama — and changed. In some way life is never seen in the same way again. It is because of such experiences that, however often disappointed, they go to the theatre in expectation, not just of entertainment but of revelation. The distinguished theatre director Peter Brook describes such occasions as 'Holy Theatre'. No elaborate props are needed, no expensive scenery, no gimmicks. He gives as one example a makeshift performance he saw in a Berlin attic, shortly after the War, of an adaptation of one of Dostoevsky's novels. Brook defines his ideal of Holy Theatre as a theatre in which 'the invisible is made visible'.[1]

Western drama has its origins in religious ritual. In ancient Greece tragedies were performed as part of a festival in honour of the gods and the themes often reflected this. In Western Europe drama evolved from the Mystery Plays. These in their turn probably originated from the liturgical dramas performed in church during Holy Week.

The connection between drama and religion however is more than historical. There is a relationship at the profoundest level of theology and spirituality. This can be seen by looking in a little detail at the liturgy for Holy Week and Easter. Sadly, except in religious communities and theological colleges, few people have the opportunity, or take the opportunity, to keep a full Holy Week. Here are some of the main features, though local practice will of course vary.

On Palm Sunday, after the blessing of the palms and reading of the Gospel story about Christ's entry into Jerusalem, there is a procession in which all the congregation take part. Originally the procession would have been out of doors though usually now it is confined to the church itself. The processional hymn is a joyful one but the liturgical colour of red indicates the Passion to come. During the service one of the Passion narratives can be sung or done as a dramatic reading with three voices for the main parts, the congregation being the crowd. It is chilling when the congregation all cry out 'Crucify him'.

On Monday, Tuesday and Wednesday of Holy Week the atmosphere is quiet and sombre. Holy Communion is said and a different Passion narrative is read each day. The liturgical colour is purple.

On Maundy Thursday the mood changes. The liturgical colour is white or gold, anticipating the Resurrection, a shaft of sunlight in the gathering darkness. At the Sung Eucharist in the evening, commemorating the institution of the Lord's Supper, there takes place the ceremony of the feet washing. A number of members of the congregation have their feet washed by the celebrant whilst the words on the theme of the Mandatum are sung. 'A new commandment I give to you, that you love one another; as I have loved you' (John 13.34). At the end of the service the mood again changes abruptly. The lights go out, the altar and sanctuary area are stripped of all ornament and left totally bare. In the Lady Chapel, however, there is a glow of candles and a bower of flowers round the Blessed Sacrament.

People kneel and keep watch through the night, seeking to obey the Lord's words at Gethsemane to watch and pray.

On Good Friday, in addition to Scripture readings and sermon, there is the veneration of the Cross, or the proclamation of the Cross as it is called today. A wooden cross is carried through the church with stops for appropriate devotion. The haunting words of the reproaches are said or sung.

> My people, what wrong have I done to you?
> What good have I not done for you?
> Listen to me.

This is the one day in the year when the Eucharist is not celebrated and people receive Holy Communion from the Reserved Sacrament.

Holy Week comes to a climax on the evening of Holy Saturday. A bonfire is lit outside the main door of the church, the church itself being in total darkness. The Easter candle is lit and carried down the main aisle. There are three stations at each one of which, on a higher note, the words 'The light of Christ' are sung, to which the congregation sings in response 'Thanks be to God'. There is then sung the *Exsultet*, one of the oldest pieces of Christian prose, with its note of rejoicing and the refrain 'This is the night ...'. While this is being sung everyone in the congregation lights a personal candle, the church becoming a blaze of candlelight. There are then read a number of passages from Scripture, each one being followed by a period of silence. This is the part of the service known as the Vigil and originally it lasted most of the night. Those who have been prepared are then baptized and everyone renews their baptismal vows. This is followed by the Easter shout of triumph 'Christ is risen'. 'He is risen indeed', a joyous refrain which punctuates the Easter season. The service comes to its appointed climax in the first Eucharist of Easter and Communion, all ending in an atmosphere of cheerful friendliness, irradiated by the risen Christ. In the Orthodox Church, the ritual is more dramatic and more of it takes place outside in the streets and in the square of the village or town.

A key element in the liturgy of Holy Week is the unforced participation of all concerned. During the 1960s and 1970s a number of playwrights and theatre companies became very frustrated. They did not want simply to entertain a well-to-do passive audience. They wanted that audience to participate in the drama and for society to be reshaped, in part through drama. What they hankered after has always been part of the Christian inheritance. Christians keep company with Christ from the procession on Palm Sunday through to the hug of their neighbour after the first Eucharist of Easter. With Christ they go through tragedy to discover joy, through darkness to find light and life. Once again they die and rise with Christ. The drama of Holy Week is one in which we fully participate and by which we are changed. The Christian congregation, the risen Body of Christ, becomes again a sign of God's intention to reshape the whole of human society.

Drama falls into two main categories: tragedy and comedy. In the Christian drama of Holy Week there is poignant tragedy. The eternal Son of God comes amongst us to take us to himself and unite us to our heavenly Father. He dies rejected and apparently abandoned by all, his mission defeated. Yet, as in all tragedy, failure also serves to reveal more clearly the values for which the defeated one stands.

Comedy has a triumphant dimension, because it brings together truth and mercy in a way that points to their reconciliation in the Cross of Christ. All genuinely funny humour contains an element of truth. A caricature, a cartoon, mimicry or satire 'hit home' because of this relationship to the truth. Yet, if such humour is not to be a form of cruelty, there must also be an element of pity or mercy. The person laughed at must at the same time be accepted. This laughter points to a final resolution of the values of truth and mercy in Christ.[2] On

Easter Sunday in some Lutheran churches of old the sermon used to begin with a joke, for on Easter there is rejoicing. Through the Resurrection of Christ evil is overcome and truth is set within a wider, everlasting mercy.

There is an inescapable anguish to life which finds expression in tragic theatre. There is also love and laughter, which also has its proper place in the theatre. Both tragedy and the triumph of love and laughter have their spiritual roots in the drama of Holy Week. Here the truth in all theatre is made visible. From a Christian perspective the death and resurrection of Christ is not simply a historical fact of the past. It is a truth in which all things stand, by which they are upheld. In a parallel fashion all genuine drama, tragedy and comedy, has its meaning in the liturgy of Holy Week. There we die and rise with Christ, there we are changed.

A large claim is being made: what those who go to the National Theatre or Stratford or fringe theatres seek, and sometimes experience, becomes visible in the drama of Holy Week. The eternal Word, creatively present in all drama, is disclosed in the movement from Palm Sunday to Easter. This large claim will sound absurd to many. How can ordinary church ritual compare with the huge amount of talent and money that goes into a major theatrical production? But the New Testament is quite clear. The usual criteria used by the world are overturned. The glory of God shines in the face of Christ. Christ is the wisdom of God. He is the tragic and triumphant truth in which all drama is to be seen.

The invisible has also been made visible in the visual arts. For more than 200 years the iconoclastic controversy raged. Many people, including some Byzantine emperors, argued that Christianity should be like Judaism and Islam in rejecting all figurative religious art. And there is some truth in this view. God is God, in his essence beyond any human representation, beyond what any words can say about him. The ultimate mystery and transcendence of God witnessed to by Judaism and

Islam needs to be preserved. But Christianity is not Judaism or Islam. It has its own distinctive truth to offer and this was put forward by the lovers of icons. First, God has made the world good, so material things like wood and paint can be used for his purposes. Secondly, God has become incarnate, the Word has become flesh. As John of Damascus wrote at the time:

> I boldly draw an image of the invisible God, not as invisible, but as having become visible for our sakes by partaking of flesh and blood. I do not draw an image of the immortal Godhead but I paint the image of God who became visible in the flesh.[3]

Although most Christian art at the time was smashed by the iconoclasts, in the year 787 at the Seventh Council at Nicaea the legitimacy of icons was established. In 843, after further controversy, the truth was once more affirmed, so that the first Sunday in Lent in the Orthodox Church is now called the Triumph of Orthodoxy and it celebrates icons. On this view Christian art is not an optional extra but an essential element in the religion of the Incarnation. The invisible has been made visible and we must make that clear.

Christianity is a revealed religion. In Christ there is disclosed both the heart of God and our true humanity. This revelation is given in and through the life of Jesus: not the bare life, as it were, but the life interpreted. The means of interpretation is given to us by certain images. These are the spectacles by which we see it. As Austin Farrer once put it:

> The great images interpreted the events of Christ's ministry, death and resurrection, and the events interpret the images; the interplay of the two is revelation. Certainly the events without the images would be no revelation at all, and the images without the events would remain shadows on the clouds.

These images are not just those of the Hebrew Scriptures or those by Jesus himself but the images as developed by the biblical writers. The Holy Spirit was active in them.

The interplay of image and event continues in the existence of the apostles. As the divine action continues to unfold its character in the descent of the Spirit, in the apostolic mission, and in the mystical fellowship, so the images given by Christ continue to unfold within the apostolic mind, in such fashion as to reveal the nature of the supernatural existence of the apostolic Church. In revealing the Church, they of necessity reveal Christ also, and the saving work he once for all performed . . . In the apostolic mind . . . the God-given images live, not statically, but with an inexpressible creative force. The several distinct images grew together into fresh unities, opened out in new detail, attracted to themselves and assimilated further image material: all this within the life of a generation. This is the way inspiration worked. The stuff of inspiration is living images.[4]

For example, in the Hebrew Scriptures God is sometimes described as a shepherd. In the Synoptic Gospels Jesus sets out the parable of the lost sheep with the clear implication of suggesting that his ministry of reaching out to the outcasts is of a piece with the outgoing of God towards us. In John's Gospel this is further developed, in the light of the Resurrection, so that Jesus meditates on the theme 'I am the Good Shepherd'.

The Good Shepherd, however biblical and revered, is a secondary image: it could be replaced by a modern image without touching the essentials of faith. There are in the Scriptures, however, some primary images of which, for a Christian, the most basic is the revelation of God as Father, Son and Holy Spirit. In the story of the baptism of Jesus by John the Baptist we have what is in effect an image or icon of this. From heaven comes the words of the Father: 'This is my beloved Son in whom I am well pleased.' It is the Son in the centre of the picture to whom these words are addressed and above him is the Holy Spirit descending, imaged as a dove. Within the life of the Godhead the Father eternally gives himself to the Son, the Son makes a perfect filial response, and the Holy Spirit — divine love — flows between them filling both. In the icon of the baptism we have a revelation in human terms of this eternal relationship.

Icons, in the technical sense of religious images, can be seen as a re-statement, in pictorial form, of the revelation of God in Christ. Although over the years there have been icons of many different subjects, in particular the life of Mary and thousands of the saints, the main twelve — the festal icons, one for each of the major feasts of the Church's year — set before us the saving truths of the faith. The icons are not there simply as teaching aids but as signs of the living, ever-present reality they represent. Through them Christ lifts our hearts so that God communes with us and we with him. The eternal, invisible love of God made visible in Christ is set before us, and we are drawn into his life.

The earliest Christian art, that of the catacombs and sarco-phagi of the second and third centuries, consists in the main of symbols. Through these symbolic representations of such stories as Jonah being delivered from the belly of the whale and the three Israelites being saved in the burning fiery furnace, Christians felt the closeness of God's saving presence amidst all the difficulties of harassment and persecution.

When Christian art became more representational the stress on God's immediate presence in and through what was represented became even more pronounced. The spur to more detailed depictions of events in the life of Jesus came from the discovery of the holy places in Jerusalem. When these were depicted the events were shown actually unfolding, together with the reactions of the onlookers. In short, those looking at the painting, mosaic or Gospel miniature were invited to take their part in the event in the immediate presence. Indeed St Leo the Great made this point explicit in his sermons when he said that the Passion of the Lord should not be so much contemplated as past as 'honoured as present'.[5]

This sense of the presence of the past was helped by two factors: one philosophical and the other religious. From a philosophical point of view it was aided and abetted by the influence of Platonism in church circles, which undergirded the Christian view of art for the whole of the Byzantine period. For those with a Platonic perspective on existence it is easy to grasp how the particular can partake of the universal, the finite of the infinite, the passing of the eternal. So what was seen in Jesus once and for all in history could be grasped now as part of an eternal reality. Secondly, this philosophical perspective was, as it were, underwritten by religious reality. God is the eternal God and through the Resurrection the life of Jesus was raised to a universal contemporaneity.

This meant that Christian art, at least for its first thousand years, never had the bare, dry historical pastness that much Church art had in the nineteenth century in Europe. It was a window through which the light of the Eternal shone now. This still remains true of icons, especially when icons take their place within the liturgy of the Church. So

> The icon is a symbol which so participates in the reality which it symbolizes that it is itself worthy of reverence. It is an agent of the real presence. The icon is not a picture to be looked at, but a window through which the unseen world looks through on ours.[6]

Icons, so disparaged as primitive by Renaissance writers and nineteenth-century art historians, have in recent decades found a new popularity in churches of all denominations and on the international art market. The modern interest in non-representational art has led us to a new appreciation of the art of earlier societies, whether Aboriginal bark paintings or Cycladic sculptures. Related to this, we realize that all art depends on a degree of convention, a system of signs. When an artist paints it is not just a question of perception, of seeing what is there. There are certain recognized signs whereby those who look at what is painted can recognize what the artist is trying to convey. Cézanne, no less than Constable, believed it was essential to look hard at nature and to go on looking. Also like Constable, he believed it was essential for artists to find their own sensation, their own particular stance. This, when pursued, would lead to a visual language distinctively the artist's own. Art must aspire to be an 'equivalent' to nature. As he said to one of his friends, 'Art is a harmony which runs parallel with nature'. All art is, to a greater or lesser extent, a parallel to what is painted, rather than a copy. Against this background, icons are not perhaps so peculiar as they might at first sight appear.

Icons, like all art, are an 'equivalent', only in their case the equivalent is human nature irradiated by God. Icons have always made use of signs: halos, elongated figures, particular gestures, emotion hidden rather than displayed, stylistic mountains and so on. There is a tradition of icon painting into which aspiring artists are required to enter. Those who come to love icons soon begin to appreciate their language. Through this language the beauty of God in Christ is made present to the eye and the viewer is drawn out of himself or herself to look and pray. Although icon painters were well aware of perspective and sometimes used it, they habitually made use of inverse perspective, whereby the viewer is made part of the scene. Their eyes are not drawn into the picture as in conventional perspective. Rather they are drawn to the surface of the icon which as it were reaches out and includes them.

Icons, though deliberately stylized, reflect the tastes and talents of different ages. There was a classical revival under the Comnenian regime in the Byzantine Empire in the twelfth century, which is reflected in the exquisite, flowing grace of the figures, for example, in the painted church of Lagoudera in Cyprus, and some of the mosaics at Daphni in Greece. There was another artistic revival under the Palaeologue dynasty in the fourteenth century which can be seen, for example, in the fine frescoes and mosaics in the Church of the Chora in Istanbul.

Icons also reflect the natural interests and curiosity of the age so that icons of the Nativity, for example, often have charming rustic touches of colour, such as the coat worn by the shepherd, or the soldiers at the Crucifixion will wear the armour of the current enemy.

There is also the all-embracing iconic element. Even when there is little classical grace and the outlines of the figures are linear and the effect either severe or simple, the icon can still make a powerful spiritual impact. All icons are a combination of the classical, the naturalistic and the iconic. What is mysterious about icons is that, though we can appreciate their aesthetic quality and be charmed by their details, their spiritual quality does not appear to reside in either of these characteristics.

Leonid Ouspensky has written that beauty belongs in essence not to the human creature but is an attribute of the kingdom of God, where God is all in all.

The beauty of the visible world lies not in the transitory splendour of its present state, but in the very meaning of its existence, in its coming transfiguration laid down in it as a possibility to be realized by man. In other words, beauty is holiness, and its radiance a participation of the creature in Divine Beauty ... The beauty of an icon is the beauty of the acquired likeness to God and so its value lies not in its being beautiful in itself, in its appearance as a beautiful object, but in the fact that it depicts Beauty.[7]

There is in fact a fundamental mystery about icons, how they have their spiritual effect. Many feel that the Renaissance, for all its vaunted advances in perspective and other techniques, lost something and this is certainly the view of the Orthodox Church. There is a spirituality present in the early Italian painters — the Sienna School, Cimabue, Duccio, up to and including Giotto — which draws on the Byzantine masters. But by Michelangelo and Raphael it seems totally lost. However superbly accomplished the paintings of the late Renaissance are, however aesthetically pleasing, they no longer lead many of us to pray in the way that, for example, the icon painters of fourteenth-century Russia do. It is stressed in all the painters' manuals that icon painting is a spiritual art, that the work needs to be steeped in prayer. But being a visible work of art this spirituality will display itself in some way. The way it is displayed is in a particular assemblage of signs, again fairly strictly laid down by the painters' manuals. But does the spirituality of icons then depend upon the capacity to read the signs correctly? It does not seem reducible to this, for many Western people respond to the spirituality of icons without any grasp of the iconography. Is it then simply a matter of taste, so that due to changing fashions we are able to respond in a way that our nineteenth-century forebears were not? Whilst we cannot ignore the role of changing tastes in opening our eyes to neglected beauties, it is not just the aesthetic quality which is involved here. It is the capacity of an icon to arouse the hope, longing, even conviction of a divine beauty coming to us within and through human beauty.

One of the most reproduced of all icons at the present day is Andrei Rublev's *Old Testament Trinity*. Rublev, who lived from about 1360 to 1430, painted this for Trinity Cathedral in the Trinity–Sergius Monastery at Sergiev Posad near Moscow (called Zagorsk when the country was under Communist rule). The scene depicts the hospitality of Abraham to three strangers, who turn out to be angels. According to the traditional schema of the Orthodox Church this scene would be painted on the south wall of the sanctuary, opposite a painting of the Sacrifice

of Isaac, both having a connection with the Eucharist. Rublev
omitted Abraham and Sarah from the scene, concentrating on
the angels. Even in reproduction the icon has an extraordinary
spiritual beauty. The guide to the Tretyakov Gallery (where the
icon used to hang), published under the Communist regime,
said:

> Adhering to the fundamental Christian doctrine of the triune
> God, Rublev endowed the three figures with a likeness and
> charm that captivate one with their exquisite spirituality and
> gentle lyricism. The angels' figures are supple and graceful.
> Their flowing gestures and delicately inclined heads imply a
> sense of profound unanimity and universal love. This,
> essentially, is the icon's emotional message which extends far
> beyond its theological interpretation.[8]

It does not go beyond that message, for that is the Christian
message. The Church sees in this scene the Trinity, and the
Trinity is a Trinity of love. It is from the burning heart of the
Godhead that universal love goes forth. We also see in this icon
the Eucharist, in which we are invited to partake. In Greek this
icon is called *The Philoxenia*, the love of and hospitality to
strangers (in contrast to xenophobia, hatred of strangers). We
may be strangers, estranged from God and one another. But
standing before the icon, before the empty place at table, our
empty place, we are invited to share in the Eucharist. This
Eucharist is the hospitality of God, of the Godhead. We are
drawn into the divine life itself, to share in it and reflect it.

Once again, a huge claim is being made. It is that the spirituality inherent in all great works of visual art, as discussed in the
last chapter, finds its focus in icons. Or, to put it another way, the
eternal *logos*, working in and through the creativity of the artist,
has become visible in Christ and Christ is set forth in icons. The
relationship between icons and other visual arts will be the
same as that between the drama of Holy Week and all drama. We

can appreciate the latter for its own sake, whilst at the same time finding its spiritual heart in the Passion and Resurrection of Christ. We can appreciate the visual arts for their own sake, whilst finding that the spiritual dimension which they suggest is actually put before our eyes and hearts in icons.

The Western tradition of religious art is not of course subject to the same canonical norms as the iconic art of the Orthodox Church. Nevertheless, it has its own witness to make. In its own way, it makes the same point. The Word has been made flesh.

The poet Edwin Muir was brought up in the Orkneys where he was subjected to a rather severe form of Presbyterianism. He wrote in his autobiography: 'I was aware of religion chiefly as the sacred word, and the church itself, severe and decent, with its touching bareness and austerity ... but nothing told me that Christ was born in the flesh and had lived on the earth.' When he worked in Rome, however, the image of the Incarnation was everywhere. In particular he was moved by a plaque on the wall of a house depicting the Annunciation.

A religion that dared to show forth the mystery for everyone to see would have shocked the congregations of the North, would have seemed a sort of blasphemy, perhaps even an indecency. But here it was publicly shown, as Christ showed himself on the earth. But that these images should appear everywhere, reminding everyone of the Incarnation, seemed to me natural and right, just as it was right that my Italian friend should step up frankly into life. This open declaration was to me the very mark of Christianity, distinguishing it from the older religions. For although the pagan gods had visited the earth, they did not assume the burden of our flesh, live our life and die our death, but after their interventions withdrew into their impenetrable privacy.[9]

The central role of icons in interpreting the spiritual dimension of all great art, and the foundational ritual of Holy Week for understanding the truth conveyed by theatre, is not meant to detract from the appreciation of art, of all kinds, in its own terms. An example may be taken from the theatre. As a young man, before he became a Christian, Augustine loved the theatre. Later in life, for various reasons, he became hostile to it and reflected how it was that he had earlier enjoyed expressing his unhappiness through watching tragedies on the stage. He puzzled over the fact that we are moved by misery in the theatre. The reason, we might say (though he did not), is that there is a tragic dimension to life, which can be captured by a combination of pity and beauty in drama.

An example can be taken from a very different culture. In his novel *Samurai* Shusaku Endo explores the difference between Japanese and European culture. One missionary in the novel, which is set in the sixteenth century, comments after thirty years' experience of Japan how difficult it is to communicate the concept of the transcendent to Japanese people. On the other hand

It was a simple matter to teach them that this life is transitory. They've always been sensitive to that aspect of life. The frightening thing is that the Japanese also have the capacity to accept and even relish the evanescence of life.[10]

This poignant focusing on the transitoriness of life is reflected in Japanese art. It has its own special beauty. Moreover, the evanescence of life is an aspect of truth which cannot be avoided. But the fleetingness of things, like the tragedy of life which Augustine saw on stage, cannot, from a Christian point of view, be the last word. That word is Christ, in his Passion and Resurrection: a death and resurrection that we share in through the sacraments of the Church, which we set forth in icons, and which we seek to live out.

This view is explicitly Christian. Yet Christian truths, Christian images, resonate more widely than the boundaries of

Christian belief. Jonathan Miller, for example, who comes from a secular Jewish background, has said that Christian imagery constantly reinforces his sense of

> The tragedy of being human, and the idea of the Incarnation is one of the great imaginative inventions of the moral imagination. I would find it very hard to think forcefully and properly without in fact being stocked with such images.[11]

To a Christian, such a positive affirmation of Christian imagery should not be as surprising as at first glance it might appear. For Christian truths are not just beliefs which a select body of believers happen to hold. They are the reality in which the whole universe is grounded. So works of art can awaken faith, or at least the longing for faith. Van Gogh said he could not look at a picture by Rembrandt without believing in God. At the very least art, in all its forms, keeps the possibilities of faith alive. Christian art makes the faith explicit.

Notes

1 Peter Brook, *The Empty Space* (Penguin, 1968).

2 Reinhold Niebuhr, 'Humour and Faith' in *Discerning the Signs of the Times* (SCM, 1946), pp. 99ff.

3 John of Damascus, *On the Divine Images* i, 6: trans. David Anderson (St Vladimir's Seminary Press, 1980), p. 16.

4 Austin Farrer, *The Glass of Vision* (Deane, 1948), pp. 43-4.

5 William Loerke, ' "Real Presence" in Early Christian Art' in *Monasticism and the Arts*, ed. Timothy Verdon and John Dally (Syracuse UP, Syracuse, NY, 1984), pp. 29ff.

6 Graham Howes, 'Religious Art and Religious Belief' in *Arts* 5.1 (Fall, 1992), p. 11.

7 Leonid Ouspensky and Vladimir Lossky, *The Meaning of Icons* (St Vladimir's Seminary Press, 1982), p. 35.

8 *The Tretyakov Gallery* (Moscow, 1979), p. 7.

9 Edwin Muir, *An Autobiography* (Hogarth, 1987), pp. 277-8.

10 Shusaku Endo, *Samurai* (Penguin, 1983), p. 163.

T E N

∾∾∾∾∾∾∾∾∾∾∾∾

Transfiguring Beauty

The almost overwhelming objection to believing that there is a wise and loving power behind the universe is the existence of so much pain and anguish in the world. The Christian seeks to live with this objection (it can never be fully answered) on the basis of three considerations. First, God has given the world genuine independence. Many of the ills to which flesh is heir are inherent in creation as such and, so far as we can judge, it could not have been otherwise. This autonomy of the whole creative process finds its conscious focus in us. We are genuinely free within limits, however narrow, to shape our destiny; and that means being free to choose what is harmful to others and oneself as well as what is beneficial. Again, given God's overall purpose in creation to bring about free, rational beings like us, it could not have been otherwise. Secondly, in the person of Jesus God himself has come amongst us and shares our anguish to the full, even in the darkness of the Cross. Thirdly, in the Resurrection of Christ we have a sign and promise that in the end God's purpose of love will prevail; will overcome all that is destructive and evil, all suffering and death. There is to be a glorious consummation of the whole creation. The whole physical world will find its proper fulfilment: 'Creation itself will be set free from its bondage to decay and obtain the glorious liberty of the children of God' (Romans 8.21). All will be transfigured and irradiated by the glory of God in Christ; all will be translucent to the divine beauty. 'God will be all in all' (1 Corinthians 15.28).

The glorious beauties of God's kingdom have often been described from the Book of Revelation onwards. One of the most sustained and successful attempts is in the *Hymns on Paradise* of St Ephrem the Syrian in the fourth century.

> For the colours of paradise are full of joy,
> Its scents most wonderful,
> Its beauties most desirable,
> And its delicacies glorious.
>
> Paradise surrounds the limbs with its many delights:
> The eyes, with its handiwork,
> The hearing, with its sounds,
> The mouth and the nostrils,
> With its tastes and scents.[1]

St Anselm was another who gave superb descriptions of the goal of humanity.

> If beauty delights you, 'the dust shall shine as the sun'. If you enjoy that speed, strength, and freedom of the body that nothing can withstand, 'they shall be like the angels of God'.... If you delight in any pleasure that is not impure but pure, 'they shall drink from the torrent of the pleasures' of God.

What Anselm brings out so strongly is the social nature of this experience.

Question within yourself, could you hold the joy of so great a bliss? But surely if another whom you loved in every way as yourself had that same bliss, your joy would be double, for you would rejoice no less for him than for yourself. And if two or three or many more had this same blessedness, you would rejoice for each of them as much as you do for yourself, if you loved each one as yourself. So in that perfection of charity of countless blessed angels and men, where no one loves another any less than he loves himself, they will all rejoice for each other as they do for themselves.[2]

Many searching questions arise in relation to such a vision. Is it believable? Is it just an escapist fantasy? (Freud). Does it detract from the proper work of changing this world? (Marx). Can such a goal, however harmonious, justify the suffering that leads up to it? (Dostoevsky). I believe that these questions have to be faced and can be answered.[3] The Christian vision remains clear and compelling: the goal of the whole creative process is a reality of all-surpassing beauty. The beauty seen in Christ at the Transfiguration, the beauty reflected in his saints, will one day irradiate the whole company of the redeemed.

Paul wrote that 'We know that in everything God works for good with those who love him, who are called according to his purpose' (Romans 8.28). This does not mean that everything that happens, happens for the best: manifestly it does not. What it means is that in every context God is ceaselessly at work bringing good out of evil and that Christians seek to co-operate with him in this way. Love, divine and human, working for good in the suffering and tragedy of human existence, is a beauty that transfigures all into its likeness. As a hymn puts it:

> Love of the Father, love of God the Son,
> From whom all came, in whom was all begun;
> Who formest heavenly beauty out of strife,
> Creation's whole desire and breath of life.[4]

A good example is given by Margaret Spufford in her book *Celebration*. She herself suffers from an extremely painful bone disease and so did her daughter. She struggles not only to cope with her difficult life but to understand all this pain in the light of faith. She writes about how in her work as a research historian the work is constantly going awry whilst she struggles to give it discipline and form. The same process seems to be at work in her care for her child. Yet things that seem amiss are somehow woven into the fabric, not entirely to its detriment.

> I know also the way in which the imperfect growths in the creation of God take on a strange beauty all their own. The twisted tree is often the one to stand and marvel at: it has been given something out of its twistedness. There is a new kind of beauty which is intrinsically painful, yet free from the grotesque. As for the twisted child, I had learnt how every 'normal' response, so hard fought for, was felt as miracle, culmination beyond reasonable hope ... The fundamentally awry can perhaps never be made whole in this life; yet like the twisted tree, or the child's courage and wisdom, it can take on a beauty of its own.[5]

The image Margaret Spufford uses is that of a twisted tree. It does not have the formal proportions we associate with a statue by Praxiteles or Rodin but it nevertheless does have a strange, severe beauty of its own. The redeeming work of love has its counterpart in art. For art is itself a kind of echo of the transfiguring music of the Holy Spirit.

One of the disturbing features of art is the way it can beautify what is terrible, can render aesthetically pleasing what should shock us. This is seen most frequently in the case of the Crucifixion of Christ. Crucifixion was an excruciatingly painful means of torture: the person died in agony. This anguish, like the anguish of those who suffer in any way, should never be glossed over, softened up or in any way made acceptable. Such pain is a horror, crying out to be stopped; totally contrary to the absolute will of a loving God, whatever may be allowed as an inescapable aspect of a created world. Yet art cannot help but beautify. A Cimabue crucifixion moves us with its beauty as well as its spiritual poignancy. A mediaeval panel in St Helen's, Abingdon, deliberately depicts Christ on the Cross as a flowering lily. What is terrible needs to be faced as such. How can such beautifying be justified? Nor can such beautifying be avoided in art, for it is an inescapable element in art as art. Seeking after wholeness and harmony is an ineradicable element in the creative process. Francis Bacon said that he painted out of a sense of 'exhilarated despair'. His Popes scream; his bodies look like carcasses of meat hanging in a butcher's shop. Many people dislike his paintings for that reason. Yet, they have their own beauty: the colour, the lines, the shapes combine to make each a painting and not just a scene of blood and horror. Samuel Beckett's play *Not I* is twenty minutes of an illuminated mouth in the darkness of the stage screaming, trying to avert some horror. The effect is so powerful that some cannot bear to watch or listen. Yet this too is art, with its own form. The Holocaust was unspeakably evil, yet out of it have come the writings of Elie Weisel and the novels of Primo Levi.

I believe that the beautifying effect of art has its justification in the Resurrection of Christ and only there. The Resurrection shows the Cross to be the culmination of a life of total trust and love. It reveals that life to be the truth about God and humanity, eternally valid and eternally present. What we see in Christ cannot be defeated by physical ill or moral malevolence. This is the basis for Paul's conviction that 'in the Lord your labour is not in vain' (1 Corinthians 15.58).

This means that the beautifying power of art, far from being a harmful illusion, is a pointer to the redemptive work of God in Christ. We can bear to look at a painting of the Crucifixion as a work of art and not just as the depiction of horror, because in the Crucifixion love is poured out for our salvation and revealed as victorious. In the light of this we can believe that all art — by giving form to the formless, shape to the chaotic, beauty to what is ugly — points to the taking up of all beauty in the victory of God's beauty. But it is only in the light of the hope given us in the Resurrection that we can believe this. Without this foundational truth the beautifying effect of art is always in danger of becoming a harmful fantasy.

During the twentieth century there have been many powerful, painful portrayals of the Crucifixion. In recent times few have been more disturbing than those painted by Mark Reichert. In his Crucifixions Reichert seeks to depict all pain, including the inevitable death of the viewer. Sister Wendy Beckett has however written of them:

> His 'Crucifixions' then are not about pain, or, at least, not only about pain: they are about the Holy Mystery, that certainty of Transcendence that takes all the pointless misery of death, and the lifelong little deaths of daily life, and redeems them. We do not know the 'meaning', but that there *is* a meaning, that we know and must know. Reichert paints this ungraspable knowing.[6]

This 'ungraspable knowing' is implicit in the work as a work of art. By its very nature art transfigures and so offers hope. This hope is grounded in actuality, in reality, in the Resurrection of Christ and all those in Christ, to eternal life.

As Christians we seek, however inadequately, to make ourselves available to God, that God's transforming work might go on through us, with the hope of a transformed world. But the world as it is continues to knock all our nice notions about. W. H. Auden tried to imagine where he would be on the first Good Friday.

> In my most optimistic mood I see myself as a Hellenized Jew from Alexandria visiting an intellectual friend. We are

140

walking along, engaged in philosophical argument. Our path takes us past the base of Golgotha. Looking up, we see an all too familiar sight — three crosses surrounded by a jeering crowd. Frowning with prim distaste, I say, 'It's disgusting the way the mob enjoys such things. Why can't the authorities execute criminals humanely and in private by giving them hemlock to drink, as they did with Socrates?' Then, averting my eyes from the disagreeable spectacle, I resume our fascinating discussion about the nature of the true, the good, and the beautiful.[7]

The Cross of Christ is the reality to which we must continually return. For this is the light in which all our values are to be seen. Our understanding of the good and the true and the beautiful is to be jarred and rejigged by the divine humility. Yet all that we value — above all the good, the true and the beautiful — has its place, transfigured by Christ in his final glory. In his poem 'Epistle to a Godson' W. H. Auden asked what will nourish a pilgrim.

> Nothing obscene or unpleasant: only
>
> the unscarred overfed enjoy Calvary
> as a verbal event. Nor satiric: no
> scorn will ashame the Adversary.
> Nor shoddily made: to give a stunning
>
> display of concinnity and elegance
> is the least we can do, and its dominant
> mood should be that of a Carnival.
> Let us hymn the small but journal wonders
>
> of nature and of households, and then finish
> on a serio-comic note with legends
> of ultimate eucatastrophe,
> regeneration beyond the waters.[8]

Not catastrophe, a final crisis with everything going disastrously, but eucatastrophe, from the Greek word *eu* meaning 'well', a final crisis in which everything comes out as God intends. Meanwhile, according to W. H. Auden, concinnity, that is harmony and elegance, has a place, as does the mood of Carnival. Nor do we need to think only of the big things. On the contrary, the small wonders of nature and our domestic life are to be hymned. In the end tragedy and comedy are both taken up in a renewed world. The serio-comic note in legends points to what will one day be the case.

The Church has not always been able to get the balance right between physical and spiritual beauty, between the beauty of God and the beauty of the world, including in the arts. In response to an inordinate, obsessive love for the things of this world shown by so many, the Church has sometimes gone to the other extreme. Yet the Christian view must be simply this: have as high a view of earthly beauty as you like, provided your view of heavenly beauty is higher. Have as high a doctrine of the arts as you like, provided your view of Christ, in the form of God, the invisible made visible, is higher.

Oscar Wilde when he was in prison wrote that 'Religion does not help me. The faith that others give to what is unseen, I give to what one can touch, and look at. My gods dwell in temples made with hands.'[9] But this is precisely the religion that God has given us in Christ. It could be claimed that Gerard Manley Hopkins was just as sensual a person as Oscar Wilde, perhaps more so, in that he was so acutely sensitive to what came by way of sight, touch, smell, taste and hearing. He relished every particular thing in its unique individual beauty. Yet, in him this was all subordinate to the beauty of Christ. His whole aesthetic nature was drawn into a unity, centred on Christ, giving him an even more enhanced sense of earthly beauty, not excluding the beauty of male bodies. Sometimes the methods that Hopkins and his Jesuit contemporaries used to put the beauty of God above the world shock us, as in his discipline of the eyes:

walking head down, not savouring earthly sights and delights. But discipline of some kind in life is absolutely necessary. There is nothing negative about this, simply a recognition that it is all too easy to pursue human goods in isolation from our supreme good in God.

As we have seen earlier, St Augustine was a highly sensual person, driven by a passion for beauty. He wrote:

> My love for you, Lord, is not an uncertain feeling but a matter of conscious certainty. With your word you pierce my heart, and I loved you ... But when I love you, what do I love? It is not physical beauty nor temporal glory nor the brightness of light dear to earthly eyes, nor the sweet melodies of all kinds of songs, nor the gentle odour of flowers and ointments and perfumes, nor manna nor honey, nor limbs welcoming the embraces of the flesh; it is not these I love when I love my God. Yet there is a light I love, and a food, and a kind of embrace when I love my God — a light, voice, odour, food, embrace of my inner man, where my soul is floodlit by light which space cannot contain, where there is sound that time cannot seize, where there is a perfume which no breeze disperses, where there is a taste for food no amount of eating can lessen, and where there is a bond of union that no satiety can part. That is what I love when I love my God.[10]

Augustine found in God the goal of all his longing. Yet he continues to relish earthly beauty in its proper place. 'Its proper place' sounds dull. Even duller is the old word temperance, one of the four cardinal virtues of prudence, temperance, fortitude and justice. Temperance, defined as restraint of the appetites and passions in accordance with reason, was regarded by the moralists as the most fundamental of the cardinal virtues because it was that on which the other three depended. Reason tells us that God is our supreme good and all needs to be subordinate to that consideration. Temperance is the virtue whereby we are able to order our lives in accordance with what this reason shows us. It means in effect what Thomas More said to King Henry VIII: 'The King's good servant but God's first.' For him this was not just a pious platitude, it meant death. So we could say: 'Lover of beauty but lover of God's glory in Christ first.' Or 'Servant of the arts but God's good servant first'.

One way of achieving this is to see earthly beauty always in relation to its fount in the divine beauty. For some people this comes almost automatically. William Blake once wrote:

> 'What?' it will be questioned, 'When the sun rises, do you not see a round disc of fire somewhat like a guinea?' O no, no, I see an innumerable company of the heavenly host crying, 'Holy, Holy, Holy is the Lord God Almighty.' I question not my corporeal or vegetative eye any more than I would question the window concerning a sight. I look through it and not with it.[11]

For most of us, however, this way of seeing needs to be learnt. C. S. Lewis thought of it as a kind of reading of experiences. He wrote:

> We can't — or I can't — hear the song of the birds simply as a sound. Its meaning or message ('That's a bird') comes with it inevitably — just as one can't see a familiar word in print as a merely visual pattern. The reading is as involuntary as the seeing. When the wind roars I don't just hear the roar; I 'hear the wind'. In the same way it is possible to 'read' as well as to 'have' a pleasure. Or not even 'as well as'. The distinction ought to become, and sometimes is, impossible; to receive it and to recognize its divine source are a single experience. This heavenly fruit is instantly redolent of the orchard where it grew. This sweet air whispers of the country from whence it flows. It is a message. We know we are being touched by a finger of that right hand at which there are pleasures for

evermore. There need be no question of thanks or praise as a separate event, something done afterwards. To experience the tiny theophany is itself to adore ... If I could always be what I aim at being, no pleasure would be too ordinary or too usual for such receptions; from the first taste of the air when I look out of the window — one's whole cheek becomes a sort of palate — down to one's soft slippers at bedtime.[12]

It is clear from the way St Augustine integrated and intertwined his reference to earthly experiences with praise to God in his *Confessions* and other of his writings that he was one who had learnt to experience the pleasures of the senses as theophanies, revelations of God, even though he remained acutely conscious that this world is 'an immense jungle full of traps and dangers'. He recognized the value of the arts, though he knew too that sometimes creative artists 'inwardly abandoned the God by whom they were made, destroying what they were created to be'. Therefore:

My God and my glory, for this reason I say a hymn of praise to you and offer praise for him who offered sacrifice for me. For the beautiful objects designed by artists' souls and realized by skilled hands come from that beauty which is higher than souls; after that beauty my soul sighs day and night.[13]

In an age so conscious of the tragic, it is difficult to talk about the triumph of God's purpose of love for the universe without seeming insensitive or unreal. It is hard to talk about the Resurrection of Christ without undermining God's willingness to enter into our total forlornness and abandonment at the Crucifixion. 'All that consoles is fake', wrote Iris Murdoch, and something within us responds. Yet the Christian can and must say something different.

Perhaps it is only music that can do justice to the dark and tragic, whilst at the same time transfiguring them into joy and

145

delight. At the end of a novel by Rebecca West in which music is a theme, one of the characters remarks 'What's the point of music with all this cancer in the world?' to which someone else replies 'What's the harm of cancer with all this music in the world?'[14] We hesitate to agree, for cancer is destructive, leading to death. Yet music can indicate a wider reality in which our hurts are made whole and all is transformed. Bach is my favourite composer, though those who know more about music than I do seem to prefer Mozart. There is a well-known saying of Karl Barth, the great Protestant theologian who wrote earlier this century:

> Whether the angels play only Bach in praising God I'm not sure; I'm sure, however, that *en famille* they play Mozart and that then also God the Lord is especially delighted to listen to them.[15]

What drew Barth to Mozart was his capacity never to hear the negative except as taken up into the positive. Why is it that this man is so incomparable? asked Barth of Mozart.

> He has heard, and causes those with ears to hear, even today, what we shall not see until the end of time — the whole context of Providence. As though in the light of this end, he heard the harmony of creation to which the shadow belongs but in which the shadow is not darkness, deficiency is not defeat, sadness cannot become despair, trouble cannot degenerate into tragedy and infinite melancholy is ultimately forced to claim undisputed sway ... Mozart causes us to hear that even on the latter side, and therefore in its totality, creation praises its master and is therefore perfect.[16]

All genuine art enables us not only to gain insight, but to enjoy what is seen or heard or read for its own sake. There is about it an element of play, something of value and delight in itself for itself. In most art the element of the tragic will also be heavily present, particularly perhaps in our time and especially in novels and the theatre. But the capacity of God to create and recreate, to order and re-order, to redeem, transform and transfigure so that the whole is seen to be worthwhile, can be captured in all art forms, however fleetingly, and perhaps above all in music. In some music creation exults in existence as such and delights in God the Creator for himself.

On the grave of Karl Marx in Highgate Cemetery, London, are carved the words: 'Philosophers have only interpreted the world, the point is, however, to change it.' Christians have much sympathy with this sentiment. The goal of the whole creative process, in the light of which all will be seen to have its proper place and purpose, lies in the future and each one of us has a unique responsibility to bring the future about. In Christian terms, Christ is risen but we await his coming in glory, when all will be transfigured in light and beauty. We cannot advance that coming, but we can prepare for it. We cannot ourselves bring it about, but Christ is bringing it about in and through us.

The beauty of that final state of affairs, that new heaven and new earth, is reflected even now in the beauty of our world and in works of art. But that beauty is above all to be reflected in our lives, for each one of us is a creative artist in relation to life itself. Rudyard Kipling wrote a poem in which he pictured everyone in heaven as an artist, each person in their separate star draws the thing as he sees it for 'the God of things as they are'. But painting is not the only form of creative activity and we do not have to wait until heaven in order to exercise our own creative power. At work, in the kitchen, around the house, in the garden, in relation to our friends and family, as we work out our political commitment to change the world for the better, we have the capacity for what is genuinely fresh, what is truly ours, for what transfigures. God is a God of beauty and we are called to share in that beauty as we share in his work of transfiguring the world. 'Let us do something beautiful for God', as Mother Teresa said.

Many of the concerns in this book are summed up in a poem by Rilke, the German poet. Rilke once looked at an archaic torso of Apollo without its head. He wrote:

> We cannot know his legendary head
> With eyes like ripening fruit. And yet his torso
> Is still suffused with brilliance from inside,
> Like a lamp, in which his gaze, now turned to low,
>
> Gleams in all its power. Otherwise . . .
>
> Otherwise this stone would seem defaced . . .
>
> Would not, from all the borders of itself,
> Burst like a star: for here there is no place
> That does not see you. You must change your life.[17]

The poem suggests an analogy with creation itself. The statue was without a head, yet the whole torso seemed resonant with personality. There was no face, yet the whole body, carved in marble, was charged with personal life. Religious people have always believed that, though we cannot see the Creator, the universe itself speaks to us of God. Its processes seem impersonal but their very regularity reflects the faithfulness of one who is constant in his goodwill towards us; the beauty of the world beckons us beyond itself to the source of all beauty. The world is charged with the grandeur of God, or as Paul put it in the first chapter of his letter to the Romans: 'Ever since the creation of the world his invisible nature, namely, his eternal power and deity, has been clearly perceived in the things that have been made' (1.20). This is not a matter of proof but of seeing, as Rilke saw the beauty of Apollo in a marble torso.

The poem also suggests an analogy between Christ and his Church. 'He is the head of the body, the Church', as Paul once put it. Or as he also said, 'You are the Body of Christ'. Christ is the head of his risen Body, the Church. We cannot see that head. But those who are baptized and believe are indeed limbs or members of his Body. The life of Christ runs in our veins. Sadly, we reflect this too little. The greatest obstacle to the Christian truth is the Church, the Body of Christ, those of us who call ourselves believers but who nevertheless obscure rather than reveal his glory. Yet, Christ is with us. Despite all our flaws and inadequacies he can sometimes be discerned:

> And yet his torso
> Is still suffused with brilliance from inside,
> Like a lamp, in which his gaze, now turned to low,
>
> Gleams in all its power.

The poem is particularly powerful in holding together aesthetic, moral and spiritual considerations. Beauty involves form; but above all it is the expression of a quest for truth, of an honest attempt to see and state things as they are, in poetry, drama, art or music. In art as in the universe, it is in the end truth that speaks to us and truth which brings us up short.

> For here there is no place
> That does not see you. You must change your life.

Notes

1 St Ephrem, *Hymns on Paradise*, trans. Sebastian Brock (St Vladimir's Seminary Press, 1990), pp. 100, 109.
2 *The Prayers and Meditations of St Anselm*, ed. Benedicta Ward (Penguin, 1973), pp. 264–5.
3 I have written more fully on this in *Being a Christian* (Mowbray, 1981), chapter 5, and in *Beyond Reasonable Doubt*, ed. Gillian Ryeland (Canterbury Press, 1991), pp. 87ff.
4 Hymn *Amor Patris et Filii*, trans. Robert Bridges.
5 Margaret Spufford, *Celebration* (Fount, 1989), pp. 77–80.
6 Sister Wendy Beckett, 'Reichert's "Crucifixion" ', *Modern Painters* (Autumn 1992), p. 76.
7 W. H. Auden, 'Meditation on Good Friday' in *A Certain World: A Commonplace Book* (Faber, 1971).
8 W. H. Auden, 'Epistle to a Godson' in *Collected Poems* (Faber, 1976), p. 624.
9 Oscar Wilde, 'De Profundis' in *Selected Essays and Poems* (Penguin, 1954), p. 154.
10 St Augustine, *Confessions*, trans. Henry Chadwick (OUP, 1992), p. 183.
11 William Blake, 'A Vision of the Last Judgement' in *Complete Works*, ed. G. L. Keynes (OUP, 1966), p. 652.
12 C. S. Lewis, *Letters to Malcolm* (Fontana, 1977), pp. 91–2.
13 St Augustine, *Confessions*, p. 210.
14 Rebecca West, *The Fountain Overflows* (Virago, 1984).
15 Karl Barth, *Wolfgang Amadeus Mozart* (Eerdman, 1986), p. 23.
16 Karl Barth, *Church Dogmatics*, vol. III, Part 3 (T. & T. Clark, 1978), pp. 298–9.
17 R. M. Rilke, 'Archaic Torso of Apollo' in *Selected Poetry of R. M. Rilke*, ed. and trans. Stephen Mitchell (Picador, 1987), p. 61.